The Rain Keeps Falling

PEONY BROWN

EXIT 26 PUBLISHING

Contents

Chapter 1

J azz Montgomery stood tall, his salt and pepper hair catching the sunlight as he guided Mrs. Thompson to the entrance of the local grocery store. The older woman clutched his arm with a shaky hand, her gratitude shining in her eyes.

"Thank you, Jazz," she said, patting his forearm. "You're always such a gentleman."

"Think nothing of it, my dear," Jazz replied, his kind eyes crinkling at the corners as he smiled. He had long been the pillar of support in this small town, and helping other seniors navigate their way around was second nature to him. It gave him purpose, warmed his heart, and helped fill the void of his strained relationship with his son.

As Mrs. Thompson disappeared into the store, Jazz glanced back at the parking lot, searching for Todd. He spotted his only son leaning against their old pickup truck, arms crossed over his chest, a worried expression etching lines on his face. Jazz sighed inwardly, feeling an ache in his chest that refused to fade. Todd's reserved personality often made it difficult for them to connect, but Jazz remained hopeful that they would someday bridge the gap between them.

"Hey, Dad," called Todd, walking over with short, brisk steps. His brown hair caught the sun like the first leaves of autumn, and his strong jawline seemed set in determination. "I finished loading up the groceries. Are you ready to head home?"

"Of course," Jazz replied, watching Todd avoid eye contact and busied himself returning their shopping cart. I just wanted to ensure Mrs. Thompson made it in all right."

"Always looking out for others," Todd mumbled, his voice laced with a hint of admiration. But it quickly dissolved into frustration as he continued, "But who's going to look out for you, Dad? You need to take care of yourself, too."

"Son, I'm doing just fine," Jazz reassured him, trying to infuse warmth into his words. "We're in this together, remember?"

Todd pressed his lips together and nodded, finally meeting his father's gaze. "Yeah, I know."

The sun dipped low in the sky, casting a warm golden light across the small town where Jazz and Todd Montgomery had spent their lives. A group of children played in the distance, their laughter mingling with the distant tinkling of wind chimes on the porches of old-fashioned houses. It was a place rich in memories for the Montgomery family, and despite the challenges that lay ahead, those memories tethered them to this tight-knit community.

"All right, Dad, I think we've got everything set up," Todd said as he methodically organized the contents of the kitchen cabinets in their new home. He glanced over at Jazz, who was carefully unpacking his cherished collection of vinyl records. The move had been a difficult decision; not only did it signify a transition into a new phase of life, but it also meant facing the reality of Jazz's deteriorating eyesight head-on.

"Thanks, son," Jazz replied, his voice warm with appreciation. "You know, I still remember when you were just a little tyke, helping me put away groceries in our old house."

Todd paused in his task, allowing himself a small smile. "Yeah, I guess some things never change, huh?"

"Indeed," Jazz agreed, gingerly placing a record on the shelf. "But change can be good too. It helps us grow, learn, and adapt."

"True," Todd conceded, his attention returning to the cabinets. "But adapting isn't always easy." His gaze flickered momentarily towards Jazz, concern etched in the lines around his eyes.

"Son, don't worry about me," Jazz gently reassured him. "I may not see as well as I used to, but I'm still capable of caring for myself." He allowed a crooked smile to form on his lips, hoping to lighten the mood.

"Of course, Dad. I... want to make sure you're okay," Todd admitted, his voice laden with emotion he rarely allowed himself to express.

"Thank you," Jazz said softly. "Your love and support mean more to me than you'll ever know."

Their gazes met briefly, both men searching for the unspoken words that had long eluded them. Children's laughter drifted in from outside, a reminder of their bond and the desire to bridge the gap between them.

"Hey, Dad?" Todd suggested tentatively. "How about we take a break and walk around town? Maybe it'll help you get used to the new neighborhood."

Jazz smiled at the offer, sensing the olive branch extended before him. "I'd like that, son." He stood up, joining Todd by the door. Together, they stepped out into the fading light, determined to face their new chapter as a family, treasuring memories while embracing future challenges.

Jazz stood by the window, observing the sunrays glimmering through the maple tree leaves outside their new home. The golden light danced across his salt-and-pepper hair as he inhaled the familiar scent of the small town they had grown up in. He could hear the distant laughter of children playing, echoing the memories of Todd's childhood.

"Son, I just want you to know how much I appreciate your help with all this," Jazz said, turning to Todd. "Taking on so much responsibility couldn't have been easy for you."

Todd looked up from the boxes he was sorting, a strand of his short brown hair falling over his forehead. He momentarily met his father's gaze before returning to the task. "It's fine, Dad. You don't need to thank me. It's just... what we have to do now."

"Still, I don't want you to feel burdened by my needs," Jazz replied softly, trying to bridge their emotional distance. His failing eyesight had been a source of tension, but the unspoken words weighed more heavily on both their hearts.

Before Todd could respond, a cheerful knock on the door interrupted their conversation. Jazz hesitated a moment, allowing Todd to take the lead. As the door swung open, the warm smile of Mrs. Jenkins, their new neighbor, greeted them, her arms laden with a plate of freshly baked cookies.

"Welcome to the neighborhood, Mr. Montgomery!" she exclaimed, her eyes twinkling with genuine warmth. "I thought I'd bring over some of my famous chocolate chip cookies to make you feel right at home."

"Thank you, Mrs. Jenkins," Jazz replied, accepting the plate with a grateful nod. "That's very kind of you." He breathed in the sweet aroma of the cookies, each perfectly golden and studded with chocolate chips. It was a small gesture that spoke volumes about the sense of community in their town.

"Please, call me Betty," she insisted, her friendliness radiating like the sun outside. "And if you ever need anything, don't hesitate to ask. We're all here to help each other."

"Much appreciated, Betty," Jazz said, his eyes crinkling with a smile. As she turned to leave, he couldn't help but feel a pang of longing for the closeness he once shared with his son. Todd was always focused on practical matters, never genuinely allowing himself to connect on a deeper level.

"Take care now!" Betty called over her shoulder as she walked back towards her house.

"Bye, Mrs. Jenkins," Todd politely replied, closing the door behind her. He glanced at the plate of cookies in his father's hands and sighed. Let's find a place for these."

"Of course," Jazz agreed, placing the treats on the kitchen counter. He knew the road ahead would be full of emotional and physical challenges. But moments like these, the simple acts of kindness from friends and neighbors, reminded him they were not alone in their journey.

"Son," Jazz began hesitantly, "I know things have been hard, but I truly believe we can make a home here. Together. We need to let our hearts guide us."

Todd paused in his organizing, considering his father's words. He looked up to meet Jazz's hopeful gaze, and for a moment, the barriers between them seemed to waver, revealing the love beneath them.

"All right, Dad," he murmured, a hint of warmth creeping into his voice. "We'll make it work. Together."

As the sun dipped below the horizon, casting a warm glow on the streets of their small town, Jazz suggested they take a stroll together. Todd hesitated momentarily but ultimately agreed, following his father out the door.

"Remember when we used to walk these streets to-gether?" Jazz asked as they strolled along the familiar sidewalks. His voice held a hint of wistfulness, though his eyes sparkled with warm memories.

"Of course, Dad," Todd replied, glancing around at the old-fashioned houses and the children playing catch in a nearby yard. "Seems like forever ago."

"Doesn't it just?" Jazz chuckled softly, his salt and pepper hair fluttering in the evening breeze. "I remem-ber taking you to the ice cream parlor after your base-ball games. You always got two scoops of chocolate, no matter how well you played."

Todd couldn't help but smile at the memory, recall-ing how the cold treat would melt down the cone and stain his fingers with sticky sweetness. "Yeah, those were good times."

"Indeed, they were," Jazz agreed, navigating the streets with surprising ease despite his deteriorating eyesight. "And now, here we are, walking these streets again – together."

They continued walking in companionable silence, the sound of laughter from nearby homes filling the air. Even-tually, they reached the local park, its lush greenery inviting them in. They found an empty bench and settled down, watching as people passed, each wrapped up in their little world.

"Look at that couple over there," Jazz said, gesturing towards a young man and woman holding hands and sharing whispered secrets. "They remind me of your mother and me when we first met. So young and in love."

Todd glanced at the couple and then back at his father. "You see the beauty in everything, don't you, Dad?"

"Life is too short not to," Jazz replied with a gentle smile. "I know things haven't been easy for us, and I appreciate everything you're doing for me. But sometimes, I wish we could sit and enjoy moments like this – without worrying about what comes next."

Todd shifted uncomfortably on the bench, his gaze focused on the ground. He understood what his father said, but it was more complex. The weight of responsibility and the fear of failure lay heavy on his shoulders.

"I'm trying, Dad," he muttered. "It's just... hard."

Jazz reached out and touched Todd's knee, squeezing gently. "I know, son. And I don't expect miracles. All I ask is that you try. Let's try to find the beauty in our lives together – no matter how small or fleeting it may be."

"All right," Todd agreed, his voice barely audible. He looked up from the ground, allowing his eyes to see the scene around them again. He saw the world through his father's eyes – filled with love, hope, and beauty – and felt a flicker of warmth deep within his chest.

As they continued their walk, Jazz and Todd noticed the familiar red-and-white striped awning of the local café. The warmth from within spilled out onto the street, inviting them in from the crisp autumn air.

"Let's stop here for a coffee," Jazz suggested, his breath visible in the cool afternoon breeze.

"Sure, Dad," Todd replied, holding the door open for his father as he stepped inside. As soon as they entered, the rich aroma of freshly brewed coffee filled their senses, causing Jazz to inhale deeply with appreciation.

The café was bustling with activity – regular customers chatting animatedly at their tables, exchanging heartfelt greetings as they passed by one another. It was a scene lifted straight from a postcard, reflecting the close-knit community that thrived in their small town.

"Good afternoon, Mr. Montgomery!" called out the waitress behind the counter, waving enthusiastically at Jazz. He waved back warmly, his eyes crinkling at the corners.

"Two coffees, please, Susan," Jazz ordered, making his way to an empty table near the window. Todd followed closely behind, his gaze lingering on the various interactions around them.

"Look at that, Todd," Jazz said, nodding toward a group of elderly ladies gathered around a table, sharing laughter and sips of tea. "People here truly care about each other. I think that's something we could learn from."

Todd remained silent, contemplating his father's words as he sipped his coffee. Despite his reserved nature, he couldn't help but feel drawn to the warmth of the people around him. Something stirred within him – perhaps the beginnings of understanding.

Later that evening, after they returned home and unpacked the last of their belongings, Jazz stood in the living room doorway, watching Todd organize their new space. The tension between them hung in the air like fog, muffling the sound of Todd's footsteps on the hardwood floor.

"Son," Jazz began, his voice strained with vulnerability. "I know we've had our differences, and I understand that it hasn't been easy for you to express your emotions. But I want us to spend more time together to get to know one another."

Todd paused the weight of his father's words sinking in. He could sense the longing behind every syllable, making him uncomfortable. The room felt smaller as he tried to formulate a response.

"Dad, I... I'll try," he said finally, facing Jazz. His eyes met his father's – filled with hope and a quiet determination.

"Thank you, Todd," Jazz whispered, his voice thick with emotion. "That means more to me than you'll ever know."

They stood there momentarily, allowing the silence to settle around them like a blanket. It was the beginning of something new – a chance to build a deeper connection, one quiet conversation at a time.

Jazz and Todd sat on the porch of their new home. The rocking chairs' rhythmic creak provided the only soundtrack to their shared silence. Jazz glanced at his son, noticing how Todd's brow furrowed as he stared into the distance. It was clear that something weighed heavily on his mind.

"Something bothering you, Todd?" Jazz asked gently, his voice a soothing balm against the quiet tension.

Todd hesitated, his fingers gripping the wooden arms of the rocking chair. He took a deep breath before finally speaking. "Dad, I've been thinking about what you said earlier. About spending more time together and getting to know each other better." His voice wavered as he continued, "I want that too, but... I'm afraid."

"Of what, Todd?" Jazz inquired softly, leaning in closer to offer support.

"I'm sorry to disappoint you," Todd admitted, his eyes glistening with unshed tears. I struggle with expressing my emotions and worry that I won't be able to give you what you need."

Jazz reached out and placed a comforting hand on Todd's shoulder. "Son, you're not a disappointment. You never have been, and you never will be. We all have our struggles, and I'm here to help you through yours – just as I know you'll be there for me."

Todd's eyes met his father's, and he let out a shaky breath. "Thank you, Dad. I just... I want to bridge this gap between us. I don't want to look back one day and regret not trying harder."

"Neither do I," Jazz agreed, his heart swelling with love for his son. "And we'll take it one step at a time, together."

They sat silently for a moment, their shared emotions settling around them. The sun dipped even lower, casting long shadows across the lawn as the world quieted. There was no need for words at that moment – the understanding between father and son spoke volumes.

Jazz let out a contented sigh and closed his eyes, savoring the warmth of the setting sun on his face. Beside him, Todd did the same, leaning back in his rocking chair as the first stars began to appear in the evening sky. They shared the silence of a repaired bond, the beginning of a more profound understanding that would carry them through the days and years to come.

"Look at that sunset, Dad," Todd said softly, his voice filled with a newfound appreciation for the simple beauty of the world around them.

"Beautiful, isn't it?" Jazz replied, his voice laced with gratitude for the chance to witness such a sight—and to do so alongside his son.

Chapter 2

Todd and Jazz sat side by side on their sun-warmed porch, their fingers wrapped around tall glasses of ice-cold lemonade. There was a sound of the hushed clinking of ice cubes against the glass harmonized with the rhythmic chirping of birds hidden in the branches above. The air was thick with the scent of freshly cut grass, transporting Todd back to simpler days when he was a child.

"Beautiful day, isn't it?" Jazz remarked, his salt-and-pepper hair rustling in the gentle breeze as he turned his face toward the sun. The mellowness in his voice always made Todd feel like everything would be all right.

"Sure is," Todd agreed, slowly sipping his lemonade. As he watched droplets of condensation slide down the outside of the glass, he couldn't help but marvel at how his father found beauty in even the most ordinary moments.

Despite his declining eyesight, Jazz seemed to drink in the sunlight. Jazz upturned his face with a serene expression, a hint of a smile at the corners of his lips. Todd envied his father's optimism and ability to appreciate the simple moments—moments he often found himself too preoccupied to savor fully.

"Moments like these remind me of your mother," Jazz said wistfully, his smile softening as memories of her danced behind his eyes. "She always loved watching the world from this porch."

"Me too, Dad," Todd replied, a hint of a smile tugging at the corners of his lips. He knew he didn't say it often enough, but those shared memories meant just as much to him as they did to his father.

As they sat in comfortable silence, Todd found himself lost in thought. Over the years, he had grown more reserved, often finding it difficult to share his feelings. And yet, sitting here with his father, he felt a sense of connection that transcended words.

"Remember when we used to play catch out here?" Jazz said, his voice tinged with nostalgia.

Todd chuckled. "Yeah, I remember. You always had a mean curveball."

"Still do," Jazz insisted, grinning. "I may not be able to see it anymore, but I know it's there."

Just then, movement across the street caught Todd's attention. He turned to see Belle Thompson being helped out of a car by her daughter, Lynn. Something about the way Lynn's eyes crinkled with genuine kindness as she patiently assisted her mother drew him in.

"Looks like our neighbor is back from taking her mother to her appointment," Todd mentioned, trying to sound casual.

"Ah, good," Jazz said, his smile widening as if he could sense Todd's interest. "How's Lynn looking?"

"Still looking good," Todd replied, trying to keep his voice casual. "She sure takes good care of her mom."

"Indeed, she does," Jazz agreed. "It's not easy, you know, caring for someone who can't fully express themselves. But that Lynn, she's got a heart of gold."

"Must be nice," Todd mused, thinking of how his father had always been there for him, even when he struggled to communicate his emotions.

"Maybe you should introduce yourself to her," Jazz suggested, sipping his lemonade as he leaned back in his chair. "It's been a while since you had a proper visit."

"Maybe," Todd agreed, unable to tear his eyes away from Lynn as she gently guided her mother into their house. As Belle disappeared behind the door, Todd knew this was more than just wanting to be neighborly. A stirring deep within him, unfamiliar yet undeniable, urged him to take the chance and reach out.

"Yep," Jazz said knowingly, pointing his glass toward Todd. "Caring for someone who can't fully express themselves must be nice."

"Sure is, Dad," Todd agreed, his brown eyes scanning the quiet street before them. He watched as a row of dandelions swayed gently in the breeze, their white seeds breaking free and floating away like tiny wishes on the wind.

The next day, Todd leaned back in his chair, taking a slow sip of lemonade. The ice clinked against the glass, a sweet harmony to the songbirds singing in the nearby trees. These cherished moments were special because his father's words weren't needed, and their hearts seemed to beat in unison.

"Beautiful day, isn't it?" Jazz said, breaking the comfortable silence. His voice was warm, like the summer sun on their faces.

"Sure is, Dad," Todd agreed, scanning the quiet street with his eyes. And then, there she was.

Lynn stepped out of her car, the sunlight catching on her long blonde hair like strands of gold. Her smile was radiant. A beacon of warmth lit the entire street. Todd felt an unexpected flutter in his chest as he watched her, captivated by this woman, now his neighbor, yet suddenly felt like a safe refuge for his heart.

"Hey, Lynn!" Jazz called out, lifting his hand in a friendly wave even though he couldn't see her from that distance. She turned at the sound of her name, her green eyes locking with Todd's. Time seemed to slow as they shared a glance, the air between them crackling with an electric charge.

"Hi, Jazz! Hi Todd!" Lynn replied, her voice melodious as the birdsong overhead. She returned their waves and smiled directly at Todd, her eyes twinkling with a mischievous glint. Todd flushed his cheeks, and his pulse quickened like a schoolboy caught daydreaming.

"Looks like you've got to do something, son," Jazz teased gently, nudging Todd's arm with an elbow. Todd chuckled nervously, rubbing the back of his neck.

"Seems that way," he murmured, glancing at Lynn as she helped Belle from the car. He couldn't help but admire the tenderness in her touch, the grace in her every movement. It was as if she had danced through life, and Todd yearned to always dance alongside her.

"Go on," Jazz encouraged, his eyes gleaming with wisdom and understanding. "Life's too short to sit on the porch with me all the time."

"Maybe I will," Todd said, a shy smile playing at the corners of his mouth as he watched Lynn disappear into her house. He had been content with his quiet life, caring for his father and tending to their home. But now, it seemed like a door had opened, revealing a world of possibilities he had never dared to imagine.

"Good," Jazz replied, leaning back in his chair with a satisfied grin. "It's about time you let someone else in."

Todd's fingers grazed the cool condensation of his lemonade glass, feeling the chill seep into his fingertips. Gathering his courage in a silent breath, he set the glass down with a soft clink and rose from his seat on the porch.

"Here goes nothing," he muttered under his breath, his pulse racing in his veins like fire. With each step closer to Lynn's house, his legs felt increasingly heavy, as if they seemed to be of lead. Yet, he pressed forward, captivated by the prospect of knowing her better.

"Excuse me," Todd called out as he crossed the street, his voice cracking slightly with nervousness. Lynn looked up from where she was arranging flowers in a vase on Belle's porch, her gentle smile welcoming him.

"Hi there," she replied, brushing a stray strand of blonde hair behind her ear. "I saw you earlier. You're Jazz's son, aren't you?"

"Yes, I'm Todd," he said, extending his hand toward her. Their palms met in a warm embrace, sending a jolt through Todd's body. "And you must be Lynn, Belle's daughter."

"Guilty as charged," Lynn laughed, her eyes crinkling at the corners. "It seems we're both in town for similar reasons."

"Taking care of our parents, right?" Todd ventured, his heart swelling with relief as he noticed the understanding in Lynn's gaze.

"Exactly," she nodded, her eyes drifting over to Belle, now settled in a chair nearby. "It's not always easy, but I wouldn't trade it for the world."

"Neither would I," Todd agreed, recalling his countless hours with Jazz. The shared burden of caring for their parents had inadvertently connected them instantly, creating an unspoken bond.

"Say," Lynn began, tilting her head thoughtfully, "why don't you join us for dinner tonight? It might be a nice change of pace for both of our parents, and I'd love to hear more about your life with Jazz."

"Really?" Todd asked, his heart leaping into his throat. Spending an evening with Lynn and learning more about her was thrilling and terrifying.

"Absolutely," she confirmed, offering him another warm smile illuminating the street. "Just come back around six, and we'll have a good time."

"Okay," Todd agreed, his voice barely above a whisper. "I'll see you then."

"Great!" Lynn exclaimed, her excitement sending a shiver down Todd's spine. "I'm looking forward to it."

"Me too," Todd admitted, his cheeks flushing as he turned to leave. As he retraced his steps across the street, his mind raced with thoughts of Lynn – her kindness, her beauty, and the electric connection that had ignited between them. He knew he was stepping into uncharted territory, but deep down, he couldn't wait to explore every inch of this new landscape, hand in hand with Lynn.

The sun cast a warm glow on Lynn's face as she leaned against the white picket fence, her eyes shining with genuine curiosity. Todd shifted his weight from one foot to another, trying to shake off his nerves as he launched into a story about Jazz and one of their fishing adventures.

"Jazz used to love taking me out on the lake," Todd began, gesturing with his hands as if casting a line. "He'd always tell me that patience was the key to catching the biggest fish."

Lynn's laughter floated through the air like music, encouraging Todd to continue. "Did you ever catch anything big?" she asked, tucking a strand of golden hair behind her ear.

"Once," Todd admitted, the memory bringing a hint of a smile to his lips. "I caught this huge bass, but it slipped right through my fingers before I could show it off to anyone."

"Sounds like quite the adventure," Lynn remarked, her eyes never leaving his face. She brushed her fingertips along the weathered wood of the fence, listening intently to Todd as he opened up about his life with Jazz.

"Sometimes, I wish I could go back to those days," he confessed, feeling a sense of vulnerability wash over him. "Before all of this" – he gestured to his father's house – "became our reality."

Lynn nodded in understanding, her empathy radiating like a comforting embrace. "Caring for someone you love can be challenging, but it's also an opportunity to deepen your connection with them," she offered gently, her gaze softening. "I know it's been hard for me and Mom, too, but we're making the most of every moment together."

As Todd looked into Lynn's eyes, he felt something inside him shift. It was as if her words had unlocked a door within him, allowing him to let go of some of his fears and reservations. In that moment, he realized how rare it was for someone to truly listen to him – to make him feel seen and valued in such a profound way.

"Thank you," Todd whispered, his voice barely audible over the hum of cicadas in the background. "I didn't realize how much I needed to hear that."

"Sometimes we just need a reminder," Lynn replied, her smile lighting up. "That's what friends are for, right?"

"Right," Todd agreed, feeling a warmth in his chest that had nothing to do with the summer sun. As they continued talking, he couldn't help but think that he had stumbled upon something extraordinary in Lynn – an understanding that transcended the trials and tribulations of their daily lives. And though they were still getting to know each other, Todd couldn't help but hope this newfound connection would grow stronger with time.

The sun cast a golden glow over the small-town street, painting the houses in warm hues as twilight approached. A gentle breeze rustled the leaves of the towering maple tree that stood proudly in the Thompsons' front yard, its branches casting dappled shadows on the porch below.

"Hey," Lynn said, her voice softening as she turned to face Todd, her eyes reflecting the last rays of sunlight. "So, we'll see you both later for dinner tonight to continue this conversation. It's not much – just some pot roast – but we'd love to share with you both."

Todd's heart leaped again at the invitation, the mere thought of being reminded that he would be spending more time with Lynn filling him with excitement and nerves. He watched as Belle, seated nearby in her wicker rocking chair, nodded her silver head in agreement, her expressive blue eyes encouraging him to accept.

"Uh, sure," Todd replied, his voice betraying his eagerness. "We would love to join you both. Thank you."

"Great! "Lynn said, her smile widening as she glanced at Belle before returning to Todd. "We can get to know each other better, share stories about our parents, and enjoy a nice meal together."

"Sounds perfect," Todd agreed, trying to keep his composure while his mind raced with anticipation. The rest of the day had felt dull and grey compared to the warmth and light he experienced in Lynn's presence, and the prospect of an evening spent in her company filled him with hope.

As Jazz and Todd walked up the steps to the Thompsons' house, Todd couldn't help but steal glances at Lynn, admiring how her blonde hair caught the sunlight and framed her face. He felt a rush of gratitude for the unexpected opportunity to forge a deeper connection with this kind-hearted woman who seemed to understand him so effortlessly.

"Mom's been looking forward to this all day," Lynn said, her voice tinged with affection as they entered the cozy living room. "She loves having company, and I can tell she already likes you."

"Feeling is mutual," Todd replied, his heart swelling at the thought of Belle's approval.

"Make yourself at home," Lynn suggested, gesturing to the comfortable couch as she disappeared into the kitchen to retrieve their meal. "I'll be right back."

Jazz Montgomery's eyes squinted as if trying to focus on the world around him—a world slowly fading away. He leaned against his wooden cane, feeling the familiar grooves of the handle pressed into his palm—the warm sunlight filtered through the curtains, casting a soft glow across the cozy living room.

"All right," Jazz said, glancing over his shoulder to ensure they were alone. I have to tell you something, Todd." The lines around his mouth deepened with concern, but his voice held a hint of amusement. His salt-and-pepper hair caught the light, adding a touch of dignity to his otherwise gentle demeanor.

Todd raised an eyebrow, puzzled by the sudden secrecy. "What is it, Dad?"

"Promise not to tell anyone?" Jazz whispered conspiratorially, his smile infectious.

"Of course." Todd crossed his heart, playing along despite his initial confusion. It wasn't often he saw his father in such a lighthearted mood.

"Okay, here it is..." Jazz paused for dramatic effect before leaning in closer. "You know, I don't like just anyone's pot roast. Haven't had a fantastic one in fifty years."

Despite himself, Todd let out a small chuckle. "Dad?" He shook his head, marveling at the simple statement that held so much weight in their family history. Pot roast had become a symbol of comfort and connection in their home, especially after Todd's mother's passing many years ago.

"Mom made a good one, though, didn't she?" Todd asked a slight melancholy tinge to his voice.

"Ah, your mother's pot roast..." Jazz sighed, his eyes momentarily distant with memories. "One day, when you're married, you'll understand what it's like to taste a meal full of love."

Todd's heart swelled with emotion. He had always struggled to express his feelings, especially towards his father, but in this moment, he felt a warmth that transcended words.

"Until then," Jazz continued, "you'll just have to put up with my sad attempts at cooking." He winked as he tapped Todd's knee with the back of his hand. "But I promise you, I'll keep trying."

"Thanks, Dad." Todd's voice wavered, and he forced a smile, determined not to let his emotions spill over. "I appreciate it."

As they sat side by side, a comfortable silence fell between them.

Todd took a moment to take in the warm atmosphere of the Thompsons' home. He could smell the comforting aroma of the pot roast wafting from the kitchen and the walls covered with lovingly framed family photos that told a story of their lives together.

The warm, savory aroma of the pot roast wafted through the cozy kitchen, tendrils of scent wrapping around Jazz like a comforting hug. He breathed in deeply, his eyes closing as he let the memories take over for a moment before shaking his head and turning back to the woman across from him.

"Smells amazing, doesn't it?" she said, her lips curving into a knowing smile. She was younger than Jazz by several decades, but a pearl of wisdom in her eyes belied her years.

Jazz nodded, ignoring how the smell seemed to tug at something deep within him. "It does. Reminds me of something I haven't smelled in fifty years or so."

"Really?" she asked, her eyes lit up with curiosity. What's the story behind that?"

Belle opened the door with a gentle push, her fingers caressing the worn wooden surface. She entered the room, and her silver hair caught the soft light of the chandelier above, giving her a halo-like effect as her eyes swept across the room.

"Ah, Belle! So glad you could make it," said a familiar voice, sweet as honey. The sound washed over her like a soothing balm, spreading warmth through her chest. She turned towards the source, her blue eyes meeting the gaze of Jazz Montgomery, his tall and lean frame standing out amidst the crowd. A genuine smile graced his salt-and-pepper beard, his eyes gleaming with kindness.

"Hi, Jazz," she replied silently, her lips moving without forming words. She tilted her head in acknowledgment, her expressive eyes conveying all the warmth and affection she couldn't express in words.

Belle felt a sudden jolt of recognition. The way he moved, the cadence of his voice – it was the same Jazz who had once been the love of her life. Fifty years had passed, but he still carried the same warmth that had drawn her to him back then.

Jazz hesitated, torn between wanting to share the memory and keeping it locked away, safe from the passage of time. But something about this pot roast made him want to open up. Jazz saw a glimpse of the man he used to be—the man he still was, in some ways.

"Well," he began slowly, his voice softening with the weight of the memories, "it's a long story, but the short version is that someone used to make a pot roast just like this when I was much younger. It was a special recipe that this person learned from her mother. Every time I smell a pot roast like this, it takes me back to those days."

"She must have been an incredible cook," she said gently, reassuringly touching his arm.

"Ah, she had her moments," Jazz replied with a chuckle, feeling the warmth of her touch seep through his skin and wrap around his heart. "But yes, she did know how to make a mean pot roast."

"Is there anything else you remember about those days?" she asked, her eyes searching his face for any sign of the man he had been.

Jazz sighed, letting the memories wash over him like a warm wave. "I remember laughter – so much laughter.

And love," he added, his voice thick with emotion. "We didn't have much, but we always had each other."

Belle's heart raced, her fingers trembling ever so slightly as memories threatened to spill over her carefully crafted walls. This collision of past and present was unexpected, but she held her emotions tightly, allowing only a flicker of nostalgia to show through her eyes.

Belle's mind raced with unspoken questions, but she allowed herself to be at ease, taking comfort in the familiar presence of this man she had once loved so dearly. She could still feel his heart even if he couldn't see her.

"Sounds like a wonderful time," Lynn said, her voice soft and full of understanding.

"It was," Jazz agreed, his heart swelling with gratitude for this moment – for the opportunity to share his past with someone who seemed to care. "And as much as I miss those days, I'm grateful for the memories. They've kept me going through some dark times."

What Belle wouldn't give to tell him everything she felt – but she remained silent, her secret safely locked within her heart. This conversation flowed around her like a river she could neither enter nor disrupt. Absorbing the sound of Jazz's voice, the way it made her feel as if she was in a cozy blanket on a cold winter night.

"Sometimes, that's all we have to hold onto," Lynn murmured, gently squeezing his arm. "But they can be enough if we let them."

Feeling a sudden surge of courage, Jazz looked into her eyes and made a decision. "You know what? I want to try making that pot roast sometime. Maybe it won't be exactly like hers, but... maybe that's okay."

"Maybe it'll be even better," she said with a smile, her eyes shining warmly and affectionately. It's my mother's recipe, and I'd be honored to help you if you'd like." Jazz looked around the room at Lynn's mother, but her face was blurry.

Belle knew she couldn't stay trapped in the past forever. Eventually, she extracted herself from the room, her heart heavy with bittersweet memories. Though she ached to share her story and express her feelings, Belle knew she must keep them hidden—for some things were meant to remain unspoken.

"Thank you," Jazz whispered, his eyes tearing up just a bit as he felt the weight of the past beginning to lift from his shoulders. "I think I'd like that very much."

As they stood in the cozy dining room, surrounded by the scent of a reborn memory, Jazz felt something stir within him—something that told him he was on the right path and that maybe, just maybe, he could find new happiness in the days to come.

As they shared the meal, exchanging stories and laughter that filled the room like music, Todd couldn't help but feel a sense of belonging that had eluded him for so long. In that small, intimate space, with the sun setting outside and love blossoming within, there was hope for deeper connections and brighter tomorrows, buoyed by the warmth of newfound companionship.

Chapter 3

As the evening light filtered through the lace curtains, casting intricate patterns on the dining table, the laughter from sharing stories about their past faded. The clink of forks against plates slowed down, signaling the end of a delicious meal that had brought them all closer together. Lynn delicately dabbed her mouth with her napkin before placing it on the table and turning her attention towards Jazz and Todd.

"Would you two like a tour of the house?" Lynn asked, her warm smile reflecting her genuine care for her newfound friends. "It's nothing extravagant, but I'd love to show you around."

Jazz patted his stomach gently, chuckling at the thought of walking around after such a hearty meal. "Oh, Lynn, that pot roast was divine, but I think moving around right now might be asking too much of me," he said, his laughter taking on a raspy quality.

" I'd love a tour, Lynn. Your home is lovely, and I enjoy spending time with you," Todd said, his strong jawline shifting as he smiled. It was rare for him to express himself so openly, but something about Lynn drew out the warmth hidden within him.

"Great!" Lynn exclaimed, the excitement evident in her eyes. "Jazz, you're welcome to join us later if you change your mind."

"Thank you, dear," Jazz replied, leaning on the table to stand up. "But I'll just go over to the sofa with my cane and rest myself. You two take your time and enjoy yourselves."

With his vision slightly blurred, Jazz navigated the familiar path to the couch, using his cane for assistance. As he settled into the cushioned embrace of the sofa, he became aware of Belle sitting beside him. Her silver hair framed her face like a halo, and her expressive blue eyes seemed to dance beneath the evening light. While she was happy to be close to Jazz, her demeanor showed a hint of discomfort. The uncertainty of when Jazz could see and his vision failed him left her on edge, unsure how to react.

Sensing Belle's unease, Jazz turned towards her, but the details of her face remained elusive. "Belle, is that you?" he asked gently, his voice soft as if attempting to coax the familiar features from the shadows.

She looked at him, her eyes full of warmth and understanding, and nodded. Her graceful hands moved with fluidity, signing her response. Even without words, her presence was comforting and calming, like the first rays of sunshine after a stormy night.

"Ah, there you are," Jazz said, relief washing over him. He leaned back into the cushions, content to share this quiet moment with Belle. As Lynn and Todd disappeared down the hallway, their voices fading into the background, Jazz and Belle sat side by side, two souls reconnected by fate and bound by old and new memories.

The room felt charged with an electric current as Jazz and Belle continued to sit side by side on the sofa. Their fingers started grazing each other ever so slightly. Jazz's heart pounded like a drum, his mind racing with a newfound realization. He took a deep breath and turned his head towards her, even though he couldn't make out the details of her face.

"Did you know," he began tentatively, "that I recognized you the moment I smelled that pot roast tonight?"

Belle's eyes widened in surprise, and she blushed a deep shade of pink. A single tear escaped and trailed down her cheek, which she quickly wiped away with the back of her hand. She mouthed her response to him, her lips curving into a smile: "I knew it was you when you moved across the street."

Jazz chuckled softly, filled with disbelief and joy at their serendipitous reunion. "Fifty years, Belle," he said, shaking his head. "Fifty years, and I never thought I'd find my Belle again."

She squeezed his hand gently, her touch conveying all the words she could not speak. Her eyes sparkled with unshed tears, communicating a gratitude for being remembered that ran more profound than any ocean.

At that moment, they were no longer two strangers sitting in someone else's living room but two hearts rekindling an ember that had been smoking for decades. The weight of time seemed to lift, replaced by the warmth of love that transcended the boundaries of age and circumstance.

"Your pot roast still tastes just as heavenly as it did back then," Jazz continued, his voice laced with nostalgia. "I can't believe I'm saying this, but your cooking might be even better now than it was before."

Belle rolled her eyes playfully, nudging him with her elbow. The corners of her mouth twitched with amusement, and her eyes danced with mischief. The familiar banter between them felt as natural as breathing, a testament to the connection they had shared all those years ago.

"Hey, no need to be modest," Jazz teased, his laughter ringing like music through the room. "You always were an incredible cook. And you know what? I think that's when I fell in love with you."

The air between them seemed to shift, growing thick with emotion. Belle looked at him, her eyes shimmering with unspoken memories, and for a moment, Jazz could see her as she was fifty years ago - young, vibrant, and full of life. Their past and present selves merged into one, a beautiful tapestry woven from threads of love, loss, and longing.

"Thank you," Jazz whispered, his voice catching in his throat. "Thank you for being here and my Belle once more."

As Belle leaned in, resting her head on his shoulder, the world outside faded away. All that remained were two souls intertwined by fate, their hearts beating in unison as they savored the sweetness of rediscovered love.

Jazz gently patted Belle's hand, a tender smile on his lips. "You know, I understand you being nonverbal now," he said, his voice laced with warmth and affection. "But Lord have mercy, you used to talk my head off back in the day."

Belle's eyes sparkled as she grinned, her fingers playfully pinching Jazz's leg in response. He laughed softly, an easy camaraderie flowing between them.

"Ah, Belle," Jazz sighed, his grin remaining as he leaned closer to her. "I'm glad to see you too. Even though today is one of my lousy eyesight days, I still remember everything about you." His fingertips traced the outline of her face, lingering over the curve of her cheekbones and the gentle slope of her nose.

As Jazz spoke, a wave of nostalgia washed over them both, flooding the room with memories of love and laughter. Belle's heart swelled, feeling as if it might burst from the weight of their shared history.

"Remember our first date?" Jazz asked wistfully, his eyes distant yet focused on something only they could see. "You brought pot roast on a picnic. I knew that day I would never be the same."

Belle nodded, biting her lip to keep her emotions in check. She recalled that sunny afternoon under the sprawling oak tree, their laughter mingling with the rustle of leaves and the song of birds overhead. The taste of homemade pot roast still lingered on her tongue, a testament to the love she had poured into every bite.

"It seems like just yesterday," Jazz murmured, his hand brushing against hers on the couch cushion. Time flies, doesn't it?"

Belle squeezed his hand in agreement, the simple gesture speaking volumes. Her thoughts echoed Jazz's sentiment, marveling at how quickly the years had passed. Yet, despite the passage of time, their connection remained strong, undiminished by distance and circumstance.

"Life has a funny way of bringing people back together," Jazz said softly, his gaze locked on Belle's eyes. "And I'm grateful it brought me back to you."

As those heartfelt words hung in the air, Belle felt her throat tighten with emotion. Though she couldn't speak, her eyes conveyed all her love and gratitude for the man beside her. Their shared past and present collided at that moment, reminding them of love's power even after decades apart.

"Remember when we went to the amusement park after our picnic?" Jazz asked a sparkle in his eyes.

Belle's mind raced back to the memory of their younger selves, hand-in-hand as they wandered through the vibrant atmosphere. She recalled how the colorful lights danced in her eyes, each ride and attraction pulling them in with a magnetic force.

"Of course you do," Jazz said with a laugh, reading her expression. "I can still hear your laughter ringing as we spun around on the Ferris wheel."

"Ah, the Ferris wheel," Belle thought, remembering how her stomach soared with delight as they reached the top. Her heart swelled with affection as she recalled how Jazz held her close, whispering sweet words into her ear.

"Never wanted that day to end," he sighed, his voice heavy with nostalgia. Belle nodded, feeling the same longing deep within her chest.

As they sat there, reminiscing about their past, Belle couldn't help but think back to the beginning – the moment their fates intertwined. They had met outside a bustling restaurant. Jazz was momentarily struck speechless by her beauty. With her heart pounding, she took the initiative, scribbling her phone number on a napkin before handing it to him.

"Call me tonight," she had urged, her voice confident yet gentle. Jazz stood there, dumbfounded, as his friends slapped him on the back and offered their congratulations.

"I can't believe I almost let you slip away that night," Jazz admitted, shaking his head. "But something told me I needed to call that number, and I'm so glad I did."

"Me too," Belle thought, squeezing his hand as they sat side by side on the couch, their love story unfolding like the pages of a cherished book. The years may have worn on, but their connection remained rooted in those early memories – a testament to the enduring power of love.

The golden light danced across Belle's silver hair, painting her in shades of pure nostalgia. She turned to face Jazz, whose eyesight may have failed him, but his soul recognized every curve and line etched into her face.

"Remember our first dance?" Jazz asked, his voice tender like a whispered secret. Belle smiled, nodding her head slowly. How could she forget? He held her close, gracefully guiding her across the floor, their hearts beating in unison.

Belle reached out, resting her hand on his arm, her fingertips lightly tracing the veins along his forearm like rivers of time. Her soft touch conveyed a world of emotions - love, longing, and an unspoken gratitude for the path that had led them back to one another.

"Your touch still feels the same, Belle. Warm and ge ntle... just like the first time," Jazz murmured, his eyes glistening with unshed tears. He placed his hand over hers, feeling the familiar shape of her fingers intertwined with his.

"Does it ever feel strange to you?" Jazz asked, curiosity lacing his words. "To not be able to speak aloud, I mean."

Belle's gaze met his, filled with understanding and acceptance. She shook her head slightly, allowing the silence to speak for her. In that quiet space between them, they shared a language of love that transcended spoken words.

"Sometimes, I think I can hear your thoughts, Belle," Jazz confessed, his eyes never leaving hers. "It's like a melody that plays softly in the back of my mind – always there, comforting me."

A tear rolled down Belle's cheek as she squeezed his hand, her heart swelling with gratitude for this man who deeply knew her. Their connection defied logic and spanned decades; now, it had brought them together again.

"Promise me we won't let go again," Jazz whispered, his voice thick with emotion. "Promise me we'll hold on to each other, even when the world tries to pull us apart."

In response, Belle entwined her fingers more tightly with his, offering a silent vow that echoed within their hearts. They would weather whatever storms life might bring, anchored by the love that had conquered time. And at that moment, as they sat hand-in-hand, their souls reached across half a century to embrace one another, promising never to let go.

The familiar creak of the hallway floorboards echoed through the living room, a bittersweet reminder of reality making its way back. Jazz and Belle reluctantly pulled away, their fingertips lingering longer, cherishing the warmth they had rediscovered in each other's embrace. Once thought to be lost in time, their memories clung to them like the dimming scent of an old love letter.

"Hey, Dad," Todd said as he entered the room, his eyes darting between the two elders as if trying to decode the atmosphere. Lynn followed closely behind him, her cheeks flushed and her smile radiant from the evening spent with Todd.

"Ah, Todd! How was the tour?" Jazz asked, quickly composing himself and sitting up straighter. He blinked his eyes rapidly, trying to sharpen the blurry figures that stood before him.

"Great!" Todd enthusiastically answered, his voice softening as he glanced at Lynn. Lynn has such a beautiful house."

"Indeed," Jazz said, his gaze sweeping over the living room. The wall photographs seemed to smile back at him, telling stories of laughter-filled days and intimate moments between mother and daughter. He turned to Belle, whose blue eyes sparkled with a hint of sadness beneath the surface. "This home seems to be overflowing with love," he continued, his voice catching ever so slightly. "I hope we will get invited over again some time."

"Absolutely," Lynn chimed in, her grin widening as she locked eyes with Todd. Their gazes flickered with something more than friendship. A blossoming connection mirrored the one Jazz, and Belle had once shared.

"Of course," Todd added, feeling the weight of his father's gaze upon him. He shifted uncomfortably, unsure of how to navigate the emotions that stirred within him. It was rare for him to experience such warmth and affection from his father, and he couldn't help but wonder if it had anything to do with the woman beside him.

Jazz's heart swelled at the sight of his son's happiness, yet a pang of melancholy tugged at the corners of his mind. He and Belle were blessed with a precious gift—a chance to revisit their past and hold onto the love they thought they had lost. But as much as he longed to remain in her embrace, he knew that letting go was necessary for now. After all, this evening belonged to Todd and Lynn and the promises their new connection held.

"Goodnight, Belle," Jazz whispered, his voice brimming with longing. He reached out to take her hand, his fingertips brushing gently against hers in a silent promise of more moments like this to come.

"Goodnight, Jazz," Belle's eyes seemed to say as she squeezed his hand in return, a wordless conversation passing between them in the briefest of touches.

Sometimes, it took a moment to remind two hearts of their love. At that moment, Jazz and Belle find solace in knowing that their story is far from over.

Todd, sensing the need to break the subtle tension in the room, spoke up. "Hey, you guys should come over to our house sometime soon, too," he suggested, glancing from Jazz to Belle hopefully.

"I think I would like that," Jazz replied, his voice warm but restrained. He glanced at Belle, who offered him a small, encouraging smile. Her blue eyes sparkled as she nodded her agreement to Lynn.

"Sounds like a plan, then," Lynn chimed in, her enthusiasm genuine but tempered by the lingering awkwardness that seemed to permeate the air.

As the evening drew close, each person felt compelled to put on a facade for the others' benefit. Jazz and Belle strove to act like mere acquaintances, exchanging polite smiles and nods, their hands itching to reach out and embrace one another once more. Meanwhile, Todd and Lynn tried to engage in light conversation, trying to learn more about each other while also navigating the complex emotions brought on by the unexpected meeting of their parents.

"Goodnight, Jazz," Lynn said, offering him a friendly hug before turning to her mother. She enveloped Belle in a tender embrace, whispering her love and gratitude for the evening.

"Goodnight, Lynn," Jazz responded, his heart swelling with an appreciation for this woman who was much like the girl he had fallen in love with decades ago. He watched as Todd said his goodbyes, the pair sharing a firm handshake and a promise to see each other again soon.

As the door closed behind them, Jazz allowed himself to reflect on the bittersweet dance they had all participated in that night. His thoughts drifted back to Belle, her silver hair shimmering in the soft glow of the living room lights, and he realized that despite the temporary discomfort, it had all been worth it.

In the end, love was a force too powerful to ignore. As they stood on the precipice of this new chapter in their lives, Jazz knew that he would do anything to ensure that he and Belle had the chance to complete their unfinished story, even if it meant navigating these uncertain waters with grace and patience.

"Goodnight, Belle," he thought, feeling her presence linger in his heart long after their parting. And with that, he stepped into the night, his heart full of hope for the future and the promise of love rekindled.

Chapter 4

The door closed with a soft click as Jazz and Todd stepped back into their home, the warm glow from the living room casting a welcoming light on their faces. The dinner date had been a success, and the memory of it left a pleasant aftertaste like the last sip of fine wine. Todd couldn't help but let a small smile dance across his face as he thought of Lynn's laughter filling the air like music.

"Look at you," Jazz said as he leaned against the doorframe, his salt-and-pepper hair catching the light. "I haven't seen you this...alive in a long time."

Todd's cheeks flushed a light shade of pink, and he rubbed the back of his neck, suddenly feeling shy. "Yeah, well, it was nice to spend some time with Lynn finally," he admitted his voice barely above a whisper. "Even if our parents were there too."

"Absolutely," Jazz agreed, his calm demeanor radiating warmth and understanding. He stepped towards Todd, searching for the right words to express what he saw in his son. "You're glowing, Todd. It's good to see you excited about something."

Todd let out a small chuckle, his eyes dancing between the floor and his father's face. He took a deep breath, gathering the courage to ask the question that had been nagging him since they left Belle and Lynn's house.

"Hey, Dad..." Todd hesitated, taking another breath before continuing. "What...what am I feeling? Is this love or...something else? It's just different than I thought it would be."

Jazz studied his son briefly, his gaze soft and empathetic despite his failing eyesight. He crossed the room and sat on the worn leather armchair, inviting Todd to join him.

"Love is...different," Jazz said thoughtfully, choosing his words carefully as he leaned back in the chair. "It can be gentle, like a warm breeze on a summer day, or fierce and passionate, like a storm raging across the ocean."

Todd listened intently, his eyes locked on his father's face as he tried to absorb every word. Jazz continued, his voice steady and soothing.

"Love does a lot to people, Todd. It makes us vulnerable, opens us up to new experiences, and challenges us to grow. But most importantly, it shows us who we are and what we're capable of," he said, his voice filled with wisdom from years of experience.

"Listen to your heart, son," Jazz added, reaching out to place a hand on Todd's shoulder. "You'll soon know what love is to you."

Todd nodded slowly, trying to let his father's words sink in. He felt a sense of comfort over him as if a heavy weight had been lifted from his chest. The uncertainty that once clouded his thoughts seemed to dissipate, leaving behind a newfound clarity.

"Thanks, Dad," Todd murmured, feeling gratitude for the man who had always been there for him despite their rocky relationship.

"Anytime, Todd." Jazz squeezed his son's shoulder before releasing it, his warm smile never fading. "Now come on, let's get some rest. Tomorrow's a new day."

Together, they headed to their respective bedrooms, their minds filled with the night's memories and the promise of what lay ahead. The light from the living room began to fade as they closed their doors, but the warmth of love and understanding remained, filling the dark corners with hope.

Belle kept thinking about this evening while in bed, and when Jazz took Belle's trembling hand in his, she felt the warmth of her long fingers and the roughness of time etched into her skin.

"Remember the first time we held hands?" Jazz asked, his voice soft and full of emotion. Belle's blue eyes met his, and though she couldn't speak, her response was evident in how her gaze shimmered with unspoken words. She nodded slowly, her grip tightening around his hand.

"Ah, that day at the little bookstore," he continued, his voice trailing as he tried to recount the memory with precision. "It feels like ages ago, doesn't it?"

Belle's eyes sparkled, seeming to hold onto the memories like precious gems. Her silent affirmation encouraged him to go deeper into their shared history.

"Your hair was a silky river of gold back then," Jazz said, smiling at the memory. "I remember being captivated by your beauty when our eyes locked."

Belle blushed, her cheeks turning a delicate shade of pink. It warmed Jazz's heart to see that he could still make her feel this way after all these years.

"Even without words, you still have this incredible ability to communicate so much with just your eyes," Jazz mused, his eyes crinkling at the corners as he smiled. "I knew there was something special about you. I knew it right away – you were the one."

A tear slid down Belle's cheek, but her smile never wavered. Jazz reached up and lovingly wiped the tear away, marveling at the tenderness of her skin even now.

"Look at us now," he sighed, gently squeezing her hand. "Time may have taken its toll on our bodies, but our love... it's as strong as ever."

Belle nodded again, her eyes shining with sadness and joy. Jazz could see the story of their lives reflecting at him in those mesmerizing blue depths—a story filled with laughter, tears, and an unbreakable bond.

Jazz felt the weight of his tired eyelids growing heavier in his bed. He fought against the urge to sleep, wanting to hold onto the thought of his reunion with Belle for as long as possible. But as his mind gradually surrendered to the encroaching darkness, he found himself drifting back through time to another day when their paths first crossed before the day at the restaurant in the dusty aisles of the local bookstore. And as his consciousness slipped away, he knew that even in his dreams, Belle would be there – just as she had been steadfast by his side all these years.

Jazz's memory of the bookstore was vivid, as if he had just entered its doors yesterday. He remembered the smell of old paper and worn bindings, the hushed whispers of fellow bookworms echoing among the towering shelves, and the anticipation as he searched for his next literary escape.

"Excuse me," a soft voice called out from behind a stack of books. Jazz looked up from the desk he'd been engrossed in and found himself staring into the most enchanting pair of blue eyes he'd ever seen.

"I'm Sorry," Belle said, her cheeks flushed with embarrassment. I didn't mean to startle you."

"Uh, no problem," Jazz stammered, his heart quickening at the sight of the beautiful young woman standing before him. "Do you need help finding something?"

"Actually, yes," Belle replied, her gaze flitting down to the book in his hands. "I've been looking for that exact title. It seems we have similar taste in literature."

"Ah, well, it's all yours," Jazz said, offering her the book with a smile. "I can always find another copy."

"Thank you," Belle murmured, her fingers brushing against his as she took the book. Their eyes met again, and Jazz felt an inexplicable connection – a magnetic pull drew them closer together.

"Would you like to grab a coffee?" he blurted out, surprising himself with his boldness. "There's a nice little café down the street."

"I'd love to," Belle answered, her eyes sparkling with delight.

As Belle nestled down into the soft sheets, she couldn't help but reminisce about their first date after that fateful encounter at the bookstore. Her hand brushed against an old photograph on the nightstand – a captured moment of a young Jazz smiling brightly at her, the sun filtering through the leaves of the oak tree under which they'd shared a picnic.

They had spent hours talking, laughing, and basking in the warmth of each other's company. Jazz had listened attentively to her words as she shared her dreams and aspirations, his eyes never leaving hers even when speech escaped her. They had communicated more with their eyes than most people did with words.

As she drifted off to sleep, Jazz filled Belle's thoughts with the rich tapestry of their life together – a testament to the power of love, unspoken yet undeniably felt.

"Goodnight, my love," she mouthed into the darkness, knowing that Jazz would always be in her memories and heart.

The sun shone brightly overhead, casting a golden glow on Jazz and Belle as they spread out a checkered blanket under the shade of an old oak tree. Their laughter filled the air like a sweet melody, chasing away lingering worries.

"Here," Jazz said, holding out a sandwich to Belle. She took it carefully, her blue eyes twinkling with gratitude. In return, she offered him another sandwich from the worn wicker basket they had brought along. Their hands brushed gracefully against each other as they exchanged their picnic offerings, and both felt an electric jolt that neither could quite explain.

"Thank you," Jazz murmured, his voice wavering while he looked into Belle's eyes. They shared a moment of unspoken understanding before breaking into laughter again, unable to contain their joy.

As they leaned in closer, their lips met for the first time in a tender, stolen kiss, sealing a bond that would last a lifetime.

Jazz lay in bed, the room's darkness amplifying his fading sight. The memory of that day played vividly in his mind, bringing a warmth to his heart. He could still taste the sweetness of the sandwiches and feel the softness of Belle's lips against his own.

"Ah, Belle," Jazz sighed into the quiet room, his voice trembling with emotion. "I wish I could see your beautiful face one more time."

A torrential rainstorm crashed outside, the droplets pelting against the windowpanes like tiny drumbeats. The storm brought back memories of another night many years ago when Belle had wanted to make up after their first big fight. But the relentless rain kept Jazz trapped inside his house while Belle waited for him, alone and heartbroken.

"Sometimes I wonder what could've been if we hadn't argued that day," Jazz whispered into the darkness, feeling a tear slide down his cheek. "But then I remember the life my family built together and the love we shared, even through the toughest times."

From his bed, Jazz could hear the soft footsteps of his son Todd as he moved about the house, taking care of things in the way that only a loving and dedicated child could. As the rain continued to fall, Jazz thought about how love had shaped his life and Todd's.

"Love," Jazz mused, his voice more potent with conviction, "it's a force that touches us all. It shapes who we are and what we become. And I'm grateful for every moment, even the ones that brought pain."

The rain began to ease, and the distant rumble of thunder faded away, leaving behind a tranquility that filled the room. Jazz closed his eyes, drifting into a peaceful slumber, cradling the memories of Belle close to his heart.

Belle stood at the window, her blue eyes wide with wonder and despair as she watched the storm rage outside. The raindrops pelted against the glass like tiny arrows, each representing another moment of separation from Jazz. Lightning carved brilliant patterns in the sky, illuminating her tear-streaked face briefly before plunging her back into darkness.

"Darling," her mother's gentle voice reached her ears, but Belle remained motionless. Her mother wrapped an arm around her shoulder, attempting to lend her warmth and comfort, while her father stood nearby, his gaze filled with concern. "I know it's hard, but you mustn't blame yourself for what happened between you and Jazz."

Belle couldn't respond, her heart aching with regret and longing. She wanted more than anything to tell them how much she missed him, wishing she could turn back time and erase the argument that had driven them apart. But her voice was silent, trapped behind the barrier of her muteness, leaving her to communicate only through the language of her eyes.

Her father stepped closer, placing a reassuring hand on her other shoulder. "We're here for you, Belle. We'll help you through this. Just remember, there's always hope. You may find your way back to each other some-day."

As the storm raged on, Belle's thoughts swirled like the wind outside. She closed her eyes, trying to hold onto the memories of happier times spent with Jazz. The feeling of his arms around her, the taste of their first shared stolen kisses, the sound of his laughter filling the air around them – these were the things she clung to in her darkest moments.

"Mom, Dad," she whispered in her mind, knowing they couldn't hear her but unable to suppress the need to speak. "I don't know if I can bear this pain, this emptiness where Jazz once was. But your love and support mean everything to me. Thank you."

Slowly, Belle opened her eyes and turned away from the window, facing her parents. She didn't need words to convey her gratitude; it shone in her eyes like a beacon of hope amidst the storm. And as they embraced her, a tiny flicker of strength ignited within her heart.

"Promise us you won't give up," her mother implored tearfully. Belle met her gaze, and though no sound escaped her lips, she nodded firmly.

"Never," she vowed silently, her heart heavy yet determined. "For Jazz's sake and mine, I'll never give up on love."

The storm outside continued to roar, but a quiet resolve took hold within Belle. As her parents held her close, she knew that whatever challenges life would throw at her, they would face them together—united by the unbreakable bonds of love and family.

The warm glow of the candle flickered between Jazz and Belle, casting a golden hue over the intimate corner table at their favorite restaurant. It was Belle's birthday, and Jazz had insisted on treating her to a special night. Though she was speechless, her eyes sparkled with appreciation and love.

As the evening progressed, laughter and clinking glasses filled the air around them. Jazz reached for Belle's hand, his touch gentle and tender. Her eyes brimmed with tears, and without a word, he understood. Time had wrapped its arms around them, but their love remained as strong as ever.

"Happy Birthday, my love," Jazz whispered, his voice thick with emotion. Belle blinked back her tears, her lips curving into a smile that reached her eyes. She squeezed his hand in response, her gratitude evident even without words.

At that moment, Jazz knew he would do anything to protect and cherish this woman who had captured his heart so ultimately. A surge of warmth spread through him like a fire, igniting every fiber of his being as he silently vowed never to let her go.

But life had its plans.

As the train rolled inexorably toward the platform, Jazz stood tall and resolute in his uniform, the weight of duty upon his shoulders. Jazz is now a draftee, and this was now his fate. Despite the ache in his heart, he knew he couldn't escape his responsibilities.

Belle stood at a distance, hidden behind a pillar on the opposite side of the platform. She watched Jazz, her heart heavy with unspoken words and their unresolved disagreement. If only she could tell him how much she loved him, how much she wished things could be different.

The train screeched to a halt, the sound echoing throughout the station. Passengers hurried aboard, eager to claim their seats before the journey began. Jazz hesitated, his hand gripping the railing tightly. He glanced around as if searching for something—or someone.

Their eyes met across the crowded platform, and time seemed to freeze. The world fell away, leaving only Jazz and Belle locked in a silent, heart-wrenching goodbye. Neither one needed any words; their love transcended language and distance barriers.

As the train began to pull away, Jazz's gaze lingered on Belle for as long as he could see her. She watched him disappear into the distance, the last vestiges of his presence fading like a ghost. And though they never got to settle their disagreement, their connection remained unbroken, a lifeline through the years that followed.

"Goodbye, my love," Belle whispered, knowing the wind would carry her words away even if she could speak aloud. "I hope someday we'll find our way back together."

In the quiet solitude of his dimly lit bedroom, Jazz sat silently on the edge of his bed, lost in thought. The fading daylight cast a soft glow through the curtains, illuminating the years of memories that filled the room. His aging hands, withered by time, trembled as he reached for a small wooden box hidden deep in his closet.

"Come to me, Belle," Jazz whispered, his voice thick with emotion as he carefully opened the box. Inside lay a faded photograph of a younger Belle, her eyes alive with warmth and wonder. He traced the outline of her face with his finger, feeling the connection to her deep within his soul.

"Even after all these years, my love for you has never wavered," Jazz confessed, his voice barely audible as he held the image of Belle close to his chest. "I wish I could tell you how much you truly mean to me."

As Jazz's heart ached with longing, Belle lay in her bed across the street, her hand pressed gently against her heart. Her expression softened as she listened to the silence surrounding her, searching for the whispers of Jazz's love that carried on the breeze.

"Jazz," she thought, "I can feel your love for me, even now. It's like our hearts are still connected, bound together by an invisible thread."

"Goodnight, my love," Jazz whispered once again to the picture of Belle, his words filled with hope and determination. "This was the day we found each other again."

The night settled around them both, their dreams filled with echoes of the past and promises of the future. And though they were apart, their love for one another remained a beacon of light, guiding them through the darkness as they clung to the hope that someday, they would get another chance.

The sun streamed through the lace curtains of Lynn's cozy living room, casting a warm glow on Jazz and Belle as they sat side by side on the plush sofa. The scent of freshly brewed coffee mingled with the sweet aroma of home-baked cookies, creating an atmosphere that felt like a tender embrace.

Jazz could feel his heart pounding in his chest as he looked into Belle's expressive blue eyes, searching for the words he had longed to say for so many years. The soft glow of the living room lamp illuminated her face, casting a warm light on her silver hair that framed her gentle features like a halo. He reached out slowly in his mind and traced a line along the contours of her cheek, marveling at the delicate warmth beneath his fingertips.

"Your eyes," he said to himself. "They've always been my guiding light, Belle."

Belle gazed back at him, her eyes shining with joy and trepidation. She blinked once or twice before offering a tender smile, her lips parting slightly in silent acknowledgment. Despite her inability to form the words, Jazz knew she felt the same way—that their connection transcended spoken language.

"Jazz..." Belle mouthed, her eyes never leaving his. There was no need for sound in the quiet space between them; they understood each other perfectly.

He glanced around the cozy room, noting Belle's family photos scattered across the shelves – their children, Lynn and Todd, smiling back at them. They were the reason this surprise reunion had to remain a secret, even with their desire to reconnect after all these years.

"Can you believe it?" Jazz mused, running his fingers through his salt-and-pepper hair. "Our children seem to be getting along... just like we are."

Belle nodded, her eyes filling with tears of happiness. She reached out and placed her hand on his chest, feeling the steady rhythm of his heartbeat beneath her palm.

"Are you as afraid as I am, Belle?" Jazz thought, drawing her closer for a goodnight hug. "Of what might happen if we let our love be known?"

In response, Belle shook her head, but her eyes betrayed a flicker of worry. Jazz knew they both felt the weight of their decision – to sacrifice their happiness for their children's budding romance.

"Then let us cherish these stolen moments," he murmured, pressing his lips to her ear during the hug. "And hope that one day, we can share our love with the world."

As he held Belle in his arms, Jazz couldn't help but feel a sense of nostalgia wash over him. Their love, standing strong through the years, was a testament to the power of their connection. They'd do anything to protect their children, even if it meant keeping their feelings on the backburner.

"Promise me, Belle," Jazz said, looking deeply into her eyes again. "Promise me that no matter what happens, we'll always find our way back to each other."

"Always," she mouthed, her eyes sparkling with unshed tears.

With that promise etched upon their hearts, Jazz, and Belle embrace, letting the warmth of their love envelop them as they dare dream of a future where their love could finally take center stage.

Chapter 5

The sunlight filtering through the grocery store windows cast a warm glow over the neatly stacked rows of canned vegetables, and Todd found himself momentarily captivated by the golden shimmer. He shook his head, clearing away the daydream, and reached for a can of green beans. His father, Jazz, had been craving them lately, and Todd had made it his mission to ensure his father's comfort.

"Green beans, huh?" came a soft voice behind him. He turned to find Lynn standing there, her long blonde hair cascading over her shoulders, her blue eyes sparkling warmly. "My mother just asked me to pick some up for her, too."

"Hey, Lynn," Todd said, surprised by the encounter. "How's Belle doing?"

"Better, thanks for asking," she replied, tucking a loose strand of hair behind her ear. "She's been having good and bad days, but I'm starting to learn the rhythm of it all."

Todd nodded, understanding the ebb and flow of caregiving all too well. "Yeah, it's tough. Some days, you feel like you're on top of things; others, you're sinking."

"Exactly," Lynn agreed, her gaze meeting his with a depth of empathy he rarely encountered. "It's so important to stay present and take it one day at a time. I've found that focusing on the little moments of joy with my mom has helped."

"Me too," Todd admitted, connecting with Lynn beyond shared responsibilities. "I cherish the times when my dad and I can just sit together, enjoying each other's company."

A gentle breeze rustled the leaves outside, drawing their attention to the park across the street. Lynn hesitated before asking, "Would you like to join me for a walk in the park? It's such a beautiful day, and I think it'd be nice to spend some time with someone who understands."

Todd glanced down at his nearly full shopping cart but nodded in agreement. "Yeah, that sounds great. Let me check out, and I'll meet you there."

"Perfect," Lynn said with a warm smile, and Todd couldn't help but feel a flutter of anticipation.

As they strolled through the park, light dappling their path from the sun above, they spoke of caregiving, their challenges, and their love for their parents. They found common ground in their shared experiences and discovered they loved life's simple pleasures: the smell of rain on a summer day, the taste of a perfectly ripe peach, and the way sunlight could make even the most mundane object seem magical.

"Sometimes I wonder what life will be like when this chapter is over," Todd mused, looking up at the sky as a cloud drifted past, casting a shadow across the grassy expanse before them.

"Me too," Lynn admitted, her eyes following the drifting cloud. "But I try not to dwell on it too much. There's still so much beauty in the here and now, even amidst the struggles."

"Like this moment right here," Todd said softly, feeling an unexpected swell of emotion. "I'm happy we ran into each other today."

"Me too," Lynn agreed, her hand brushing against his as they walked side by side, their hearts beating in unison to the tender rhythm of a newfound connection.

Leaves crunched under their feet as Todd and Lynn walked through the park, the vibrant autumn colors surrounding them like a warm embrace. The trees swayed gently in the breeze, their branches dancing shadows on the ground below.

"Sometimes I feel so guilty," Lynn admitted, her voice barely above a whisper, laden with emotion. "I want to be there for my mom, but it can be draining."

Todd nodded, his eyes cast downward as he mulled over her words. "I know what you mean. It's a constant battle between wanting to help them and needing to take care of ourselves, too." He sighed, feeling the weight of their shared burden.

Lynn looked over at him, her eyes shining with empathy. "It's comforting to know someone else understands, however. It makes me feel less alone."

"Same here," Todd agreed, offering a smile. As they continued walking, he felt a newfound sense of camaraderie with Lynn, a connection beyond their initial meeting.

"Hey," Todd said suddenly, spotting a nearby café. "Would you like to grab some coffee? We could continue our conversation there."

"Sure, that sounds lovely," Lynn replied, her eyes lighting up at the suggestion.

As they settled into the cozy corner of the quaint café, the aroma of freshly brewed coffee enveloping them, Todd and Lynn began exchanging stories about their parents' quirks and idiosyncrasies.

"Jazz has this habit of whistling old tunes from his youth," Todd shared, chuckling. "He'll whistle the same tune all day until it's stuck in my head, too."

Lynn laughed, her eyes crinkling at the corners as she imagined the scene. "My mom does something similar. She hums while she cooks, but she always seems to forget half the melody. So, you end up with this strange mix of songs that don't quite fit together."

"Sounds like our parents should get along," Todd said, his laughter mingling with Lynn's.

As they shared more stories and continued their conversation, Todd couldn't help but feel a sense of warmth and belonging. In Lynn, he had found a kindred spirit and someone who truly understood the depth of his emotions and experiences. As they sipped their coffee, their hands occasionally brushing against each other, Todd allowed himself to entertain the possibility of a more profound connection beyond the bonds of shared caregiving and fears.

The sun dipped below the horizon, casting a warm, golden hue over the café as Todd and Lynn lingered over their coffee. The laughter from their shared stories still hung in the air like a comforting embrace. Todd took a deep breath, inhaling the rich scent of coffee beans mixed with the faint perfume of the nearby flower shop, and felt a sense of contentment he hadn't experienced in years.

"Speaking of cooking," Lynn began, her fingers tracing the rim of her coffee cup, "my mom loves preparing meals for people. She used to make these incredible feasts when I was growing up. Of course, her pot roast was legendary in our neighborhood."

Todd's eyes widened, his mouth watering at the mere thought of a home-cooked meal. It had been ages since he'd enjoyed something other than his rudimentary cooking skills. His father's deteriorating vision had made it difficult for Jazz to prepare anything more complex than a sandwich.

"Would you and your father be interested in having my mom come over and cook for you sometime?" Lynn asked hesitantly, her cheeks flushed with enthusiasm and vulnerability. "She hasn't had much reason to cook big meals lately. She would enjoy it, which might differ from her famous pot roast."

"Really? That sounds amazing!" Todd exclaimed, warmth spreading through his chest at the thought of spending more time with Lynn and getting to know her mother. He imagined the savory scents wafting through the house, intermingling with laughter and conversation. "While Belle's cooking, maybe she could even teach my dad a thing or two in the kitchen. He used to love cooking but hasn't been able to do much since his eyesight started to decline."

Lynn's eyes sparkled as she nodded her agreement, excited by the prospect. "I'm sure they'd both enjoy that," she said, a soft smile tugging at the corners of her mouth. "It might be a nice change for both of them."

At that moment, sitting across from Lynn in the amber glow of the setting sun, Todd felt a swell of anticipation for the future. There was something magnetic about her presence, pulling him closer with each shared experience and heartfelt conversation. As they planned an evening with their parents, he couldn't help but wonder if this newfound connection could grow into something more profound and lasting.

"Let's do it," Todd said, his voice filled with conviction and hope. "Let's give our parents a night to remember and see where this journey takes all of us."

Lynn's fingers brushed against his as their eyes met, and in that instant, they both knew that whatever lay ahead, they would face it side by side.

The evening air was crisp and fragrant, carrying the scent of freshly bloomed flowers as Lynn and Belle approached Jazz and Todd's house. The porch light cast a warm glow, illuminating their path as they carried a bottle of wine between them – a small token of appreciation for the invitation.

Todd spotted them from inside the house and quickly opened the door, his face lighting up with a genuine smile. "Lynn, Belle, welcome!" he said, ushering them inside. As they crossed the threshold, the cozy atmosphere of the home enveloped them like a soft embrace.

"Thank you for having us, Todd," Lynn said, handing him the wine. "We thought this would be a nice addition to dinner."

"Ah, perfect choice," Todd replied, admiring the label before placing it on the counter. "Please, make yourselves at home."

Belle, communicating her gratitude through her expressive eyes, nodded and unpacked the ingredients she had brought. Her hands moved gracefully, revealing years of experience in the kitchen. Jazz shuffled in, leaning on his cane, and watched her with curiosity and admiration.

"Need any help, Belle?" he asked, his voice tender as he navigated the space despite his impaired vision.

Belle shook her head, giving him a reassuring smile as she continued to work her magic on the meal. Not a person to be deterred by anything, Jazz followed her every move like a smitten teenager, his enthusiasm undiminished by age or circumstance.

Meanwhile, Todd and Lynn settled into the living room, laughter bubbling between them as they exchanged stories and shared memories. "So, your mother is quite the chef, huh?" Todd remarked, stealing a glance at the bustling kitchen.

"Absolutely," Lynn agreed, grinning. "I swear, food tastes better when she makes it. It's like she infuses each dish with love."

Todd chuckled, his eyes crinkling at the corners. "I can't wait to experience it myself. And I'm glad my dad has someone to learn from, too. He hasn't been in the kitchen much since..."

"Since his eyesight started to decline?" Lynn finished gently, her hand reaching for his. Todd nodded, grateful for her understanding.

"Exactly," he said softly, gently squeezing her hand. "But tonight feels like a new beginning for all of us."

As the aroma of home-cooked food filled the air and laughter echoed through the house, Todd and Lynn's connection grew. Each shared moment brought them closer together, weaving a tapestry of friendship and affection that seemed destined to last.

As the evening progressed, the dining room table filled with laughter, clinking glasses, and stories shared between bites of Belle's exquisite cooking. The warm glow of candlelight danced across the faces of Jazz, Todd, Lynn, and Belle, casting a spell of contentment over the gathering.

"Mom, this is fantastic," Lynn praised between mouthfuls. "You've truly outdone yourself."

"Agreed," Todd chimed in, his eyes twinkling with appreciation. "I haven't had food this good since... well, I can't even remember."

Belle beamed at their compliments, her eyes shining with pride. Her gaze drifted around the room, eventually settling on an old photograph that hung on the wall. It depicted a young Jazz in his military uniform, standing tall with determination.

She rose from her seat and approached the photo, her movements unhurried and graceful. As Belle studied the image before her, Lynn couldn't help but notice her mother's captivated expression.

"Ah, your dad in his younger years," Lynn remarked, nodding toward the photograph. "Moms always had a thing for men in uniform."

"Is that so?" Jazz asked, a nostalgic smile on his lips as he followed Belle to the picture. His cane tapped lightly against the floor, guiding him through the shadows. Drawing close to Belle, he spoke as though sharing a secret. "I'll never forget the day that photo was taken. Waiting on that train platform, ready to leave everything behind, or at least I thought..."

He trailed off, his eyes clouded with recollections. Belle's eyes held a knowing glimmer, communicating her understanding of the moment he described. She wanted to reach for his hand but gently squeezed her own in silent support.

"I understand," Jazz whispered, his voice barely audible. "I understand."

Todd observed the exchange between his father and Belle, feeling a strange sense of familiarity. Though he couldn't quite grasp it, their connection seemed to transcend time and circumstance.

"Your mother is an extraordinary woman," Jazz said as he returned to the table, addressing Lynn with a fond smile. "I'm grateful for her presence here tonight."

"Thank you, Mr. Montgomery," Lynn replied, returning the smile. "And so are we."

As the evening wore on, Todd couldn't help but notice something budding between his father and Belle. Even though his heart swelled with joy at the thought of their happiness, he was determined not to let anything over-shadow the growing bond between himself and Lynn.

"Here's to new beginnings," he proposed, raising his glass in a toast. The others raised theirs, and each person lost in their thoughts and hopes for the future.

"New beginnings," they echoed in unison, sealing the promise with a sip of wine.

The clattering of dishes and silverware filled the air as Todd and Lynn cleared the dining table after dinner. The faint scent of the home-cooked meal lingered in the room, a warm embrace that refused to let go. As they carried their armfuls of plates into the kitchen, Lynn offered her help with the monumental task of cleaning up.

"Let's tackle these dishes together," she suggested, her voice soft yet resolute. "It'll be faster and more enjoyable."

"Thanks, Lynn. I appreciate it," Todd replied, his eyes meeting hers briefly before focusing on the soapy water filling the sink. He couldn't deny the comfort he felt in her presence, a feeling that was both foreign and familiar.

As they scrubbed away at the remnants of the feast, Lynn asked Todd about Jazz and Belle. "Do you think our parents could have found a new friend in each other?" she inquired, her tone gentle and curious.

Todd glanced over at Jazz and Belle, who were now seated in the living room, conversing quietly with one another. The warmth and ease between them was undeniable. "I hope so," he admitted, his shoulders relaxing slightly. "They seem to have something special – just like us."

Lynn smiled at his words, her heart swelling with happiness. "I'm glad we had this chance to connect, Todd. It's been such a lovely evening."

"Me too, Lynn. Me too." Todd paused, his hands submerged in sudsy water, as he considered the depth of his feelings for Lynn. The realization struck him like a lightning bolt – he wanted to explore a deeper connection with her and share life's beauty and pain.

Todd turned to face Belle, who was observing them from her spot on the couch. Her blue eyes seemed to hold an ocean of wisdom and understanding. "Thank you, Belle," he said with sincerity, his voice thick with emotion. "I promise to cherish your daughter and be there for her, just as she has been for me."

Belle's gaze shifted to Jazz, a silent nod of approval passing between them. She believed Todd would honor his word and that Jazz had raised a son worthy of her daughter's love.

"Let's finish here," Lynn gently urged, sensing the moment's weight. "We can join our parents in the living room and enjoy the rest of the evening together."

Todd nodded, his heart full and hopeful. As they dried the last dish and placed it on the rack, he felt overwhelming gratitude for this newfound connection. The future stretched before them, brimming with possibilities and the promise of love.

The living room's warmth seemed to wrap around them like a soft, welcoming embrace as they prepared to say goodbye. Todd couldn't help but notice how Lynn's eyes sparkled in the dimly lit space, reflecting the flickering glow of the mantel's candles.

"Thank you for such a wonderful evening," Lynn said, her voice barely above a whisper. "It was nice to spend time together and get to know each other better."

"Likewise," Todd replied, trying to maintain his composure. "I enjoyed our conversation and... well, everything." He could feel the heat rising in his cheeks as he fought to contain the overwhelming emotions surging.

They stood facing one another for a moment, the air charged with unspoken sentiments between them. Neither wanted to be the first to break the silence, fearing it would shatter the delicate connection they had forged throughout the night.

Belle and Jazz emerged from the kitchen, sensing the time had come for their departure. "We'd best be going. Belle communicated with a gentle smile and a nod towards the door.

"Let us walk you home," Jazz insisted, his deep voice hinting at nostalgia and tenderness. "It's getting dark out, and we want to ensure you get back safely."

"Thank you," Lynne replied, touched by the men's gesture of care.

As they stepped out into the crisp night air, the stars overhead seemed to dance to celebrate their newfound bond. The short walk across the street felt familiar and exciting as if they were embarking on a new adventure together.

Todd's heart swelled with hope and anticipation, his thoughts consumed by the possibility of a future with Lynn. As they walked, he glanced over at his father, who was walking close beside Belle. Something in the way Jazz looked at her – a mixture of reverence and curiosity – made Todd wonder about the hidden depths of their connection. He let it unfold naturally, trusting that whatever story lay between them would reveal itself.

"Here we are," Lynn said as they reached her front door. "Thank you again for tonight. I had a great time."

"Me too," Todd confessed, his voice catching with emotion. "I'm looking forward to getting to know you even better."

"Goodnight, Todd," Lynn whispered, her eyes lingering on his face for a moment longer before she turned to enter her home.

"Goodnight, Lynn," he managed to reply, the words heavy with unspoken affection.

With a final wave, Belle and Lynn disappeared behind their front door, leaving Jazz and Todd on the sidewalk, their minds awash with thoughts of love and possibility. As they turned to walk back to their home, the night seemed to hold a promise, not only for the two hearts that had begun to intertwine but also for the generations past and those yet to come.

The soft glow of the streetlamp cast a warm light on Jazz and Todd as they began their walk back home. The gentle hum of crickets in the summer night enveloped them, creating a serene atmosphere reflecting the emotions stirring within their hearts.

"Quite an evening, huh?" Jazz said, breaking the silence with a hint of nostalgia in his voice.

"It was," Todd replied, recalling the laughter and heartfelt conversations he shared with Lynn. "I haven't felt this... alive in a long time."

"Life has a way of surprising us when we least expect it," Jazz mused, inhaling the sweet scent of jasmine that lingered in the air.

"Did you notice something between you and Belle?" Todd asked hesitantly, still trying to make sense of the connection he had observed between the two earlier in the evening.

"Maybe," Jazz admitted, a faraway look in his eyes. "It's hard to put my finger on it, but there's something familiar about her. Like a song I forgot I loved."

"Whatever it is," Todd said with genuine warmth, "I'm happy for you, Dad."

"Thank you, son." Jazz placed a hand on Todd's shoulder, squeezing gently. "And what about you and Lynn? You seemed to hit it off quite well."

"Something just clicked between us," Todd confessed, feeling his chest swell with emotion. "I don't know what it means, but I want to find out."

"Take your time," Jazz advised, a knowing smile playing at the corners of his lips. "You deserve to be happy too, Todd. We all do."

As they continued walking, Todd's thoughts returned to the tender moments he'd shared with Lynn. Her laughter was like a melody that resonated deep within him; the sincerity in her eyes when she spoke of her mother; the way her hand felt in his, warm and steady like an anchor.

"Any advice for a hopeless romantic?" Todd asked with a chuckle, seeking wisdom from his father's years of experience.

"Trust your heart," Jazz replied simply. "It knows the way."

A comfortable silence settled between them once more as they approached their home, the front porch light casting a warm glow that beckoned them inside. As they stepped through the door, both men couldn't help but feel the world had shifted ever so slightly beneath their feet, opening the door to new possibilities and uncharted territory.

"Goodnight, Dad," Todd whispered, pausing at the foot of the stairs.

"Goodnight, son," Jazz responded, his voice laced with gratitude and hope. "Sweet dreams."

As Todd ascended the stairs, he thought of Lynn, her eyes shining like stars in the night sky, and allowed himself to believe that perhaps, just perhaps, love could be waiting on the horizon.

Chapter 6

The sun dipped low on the horizon, casting a warm golden glow over Jazz Montgomery's porch. He sat in his worn rocking chair, its creaks syncing with the rhythm of his movements. Beside him, Ray Williams lounged on an equally aged loveseat, both men sipping on cold lemonade—a perfect antidote to the sweltering summer heat.

"Ray, I've been meaning to talk to you about something," Jazz began, his hesitant voice tinged with excitement. "It's about Belle."

Ray leaned forward, his expressive eyes narrowing with curiosity. "What about her?"

"She lives across the street. I can't help but feel all these emotions bubbling inside me—emotions I thought I had buried deep down."

Jazz paused, his gaze drifting across the lawn to where the Thompson house stood. Through the waning sunlight, he saw Belle's silhouette moving gracefully behind her living room window curtains. His heart fluttered at the sight.

"Go on," Ray urged gently, placing his glass on the small table between them and clasping his hands together. "I'm listening."

"Seeing Belle again after all these years has stirred up feelings I never thought I'd experience again. It's... it's hard to put into words."

"Love's like that, isn't it?" Ray mused, casting a knowing glance at his friend. "It sneaks up on you when you least expect it."

"Is it love, though?" Jazz questioned, his salt-and-pepper brows furrowing. "Or is it just nostalgia for a time when we were younger and life was simpler?"

"There's only one way to find out, my friend," Ray chuckled. You've got to dive in and explore it."

"But what if it's a mistake?" Jazz's voice trembled as the weight of his own words settled upon him.

"Jazz, listen." Ray leaned in closer, his eyes earnest and filled with empathy. "We've all made mistakes in our lives. But those very mistakes have led us to where we are today. You can't let fear hold you back."

"Maybe you're right," Jazz conceded, his thoughts turning inward as he considered Ray's advice. He sipped on his lemonade, the bittersweet tang a fitting reflection of his emotions.

"Trust me, I know a thing or two about love," Ray said with a wink, the corners of his eyes crinkling as a warm smile spread across his face. "Take it from someone who's been around the block a few times: you'll never know unless you try."

"Thank you, Ray," Jazz murmured, grateful for his friend's support and understanding.

"Any time, Jazz. Any time."

A gentle breeze rustled the leaves of the surrounding trees, adding a soothing melody to their conversation. The lemonade in their glasses shimmered like liquid amber, its sweet tang lingering on their lips.

"Ray," Jazz began, his voice wavering with uncertainty, "what if pursuing this second chance with Belle only leads to disappointment for both of us? I can't bear the thought of causing her pain or opening my heart to have it broken again."

Ray leaned back in his chair, studying Jazz's face momentarily before speaking. "Jazz, when my wife passed away, I thought I'd never find love again. It hurt too much even to consider letting someone else in." He took a deep breath, his gaze drifting into the distance as he recalled the memory. "But then I met someone who made me realize that love is always worth the risk. You see, life is too short to let fear dictate our choices."

Jazz looked at his friend, taking in the sincerity etched on Ray's face. He felt a surge of gratitude for Ray's openness, knowing that delving into these emotions couldn't be easy for him.

"Did you... ever regret taking that risk?" Jazz asked tentatively, curiosity mingling with the trepidation that tightened his chest.

"Regret?" Ray shook his head, a bittersweet smile tugging at the corners of his mouth. "No, Jazz. There were times when it was difficult and moments of heartache. But ultimately, I found happiness in the most unexpected places."

"Even after loss?" Jazz pressed, his hands clasping tightly as his heart ached with hope and fear.

"Especially after loss," Ray confirmed, giving Jazz a reassuring and understanding nod. "Because it's in those moments when we feel most vulnerable that we're reminded of what truly matters."

Jazz mulled over Ray's words, feeling their weight settle within him like a warm embrace. He knew his friend was right – love would always involve risks, but the potential rewards were immeasurable. Jazz felt a quiet determination stir within his soul as the sun continued to sink toward the horizon, casting long shadows across the porch.

"Thank you, Ray," he said, his voice filled with newfound resolve. "I think... I think I'm ready to take that leap."

Ray clapped him on the shoulder, his eyes twinkling with pride and affection. "That's the spirit, Jazz. Remember, sometimes the greatest adventures begin with a single step."

As the final rays of sunlight disappeared behind the trees, Jazz took a deep breath, savoring the scent of the approaching night. The world seemed suddenly filled with infinite possibilities, and though uncertainty still lingered, he knew he could face it head-on – with Belle by his side.

Jazz gazed at the fireflies, their tiny lights flickering like stars in the twilight. Each little flash seemed to spark a memory - of shared laughter, tears shed, and love lost and found again. He took a deep breath, inhaling the sweet scent of honeysuckle that clung to the warm evening air.

"Ray's right," Jazz whispered, his knuckles white as he gripped the porch railing. "Life's too short to let fear hold me back."

He turned his thoughts to Belle, her silver hair reflecting the moonlight, her blue eyes filled with unspoken words. He thought of how she'd looked at him when they were young, as if he was the only one who mattered. And now, after all these years apart, could he find the courage to try again?

"Jazz, is everything all right?" Maggie asked, appearing from around the corner of the neighboring house. Her curly red hair framed her face, a picture of concern etched upon it.

"Ah, yes, I'm fine, Maggie," Jazz replied, forcing a smile. "Just enjoying this beautiful evening."

"Good," she said, nodding in satisfaction. "Belle's out back in the garden with me if you want to join us."

"Maybe in a bit," he said, offering her a grateful nod.

"Take your time," Maggie responded before returning to the garden.

Jazz knew that Belle must have felt just as conflicted as he did. As he watched Maggie slip away, he realized that Belle had sought solace in their friendship. Maggie had always been able to communicate with Belle despite her muteness—a skill that came from years of understanding and empathy.

"Your heart will guide you," Ray echoed in Jazz's mind. "Love will always involve risks, but the potential rewards are immeasurable."

Jazz's heart swelled warmly, and he knew what to do. It was time to take that leap of faith - for Belle, himself, and the love still burning brightly within them both.

He strode through the garden, feeling the damp grass beneath his feet as the fireflies danced around him. He could see Maggie and Belle sitting on a wooden bench, their faces illuminated by the soft glow of a lantern. As Jazz approached, Belle turned her head, her eyes meeting his.

"I just wanted to say hello, and you ladies have a beautiful evening," Jazz said, his voice strong and steady.

"Please sit with us," Maggie answered, patting the space beside her.

As Jazz stood there thinking, he felt the familiar warmth of Belle's presence wash over him. Their eyes locked for a moment, sharing a silent understanding. One thought resonated in his mind: life is too short to let fear hold him back from happiness.

"Maybe next time," Jazz said, his voice barely above a whisper. "It's been a long time."

The sun cast a warm, golden light across the garden as Belle and Maggie sat on a cozy wooden bench, a weathered scrapbook opened between them. The air was filled with the sweet scent of blooming roses and the gentle hum of bees buzzing among the flowers. A soft breeze played with Belle's silver hair as her eyes danced over the photographs from years ago.

"Look at this one," Maggie said, pointing to a picture of a young Jazz and Belle, their arms around each other, grinning ear-to-ear. "You two were just inseparable back then, weren't you?"

Belle nodded, her blue eyes misting over with nostalgia. She traced her fingers along the edge of the photograph, feeling the rough texture of the aged paper beneath her fingertips.

"Remember that summer?" Maggie asked, her voice tinged with the warmth of shared memories. "You two could barely keep your hands off each other, always sneaking kisses in the garden when you thought no one was looking."

A blush spread across Belle's cheeks, and she smiled shyly, recalling those stolen moments of passion. The joy from those memories swirled within her, tempered by a longing for what once was.

Maggie flipped through the scrapbook pages, pausing at another photo - this time, Belle cradled a newborn baby, her face alight with happiness. Belle's eyes lingered on the image, her heart swelling with love and pride for her family and daughter Lynn.

"Your love for your daughter was always so strong," Maggie said, gently squeezing Belle's hand. "It's still a beautiful thing to witness."

As the memories continued to flow, Belle felt her chest tighten with emotion. As much as she cherished the past, she couldn't help but feel the weight of the unspoken words, the lost opportunities that hung between her and Jazz. She looked up from the scrapbook, meeting Maggie's compassionate gaze.

"Is something on your mind, dear?" Maggie asked, her eyes searching Belle's face for an answer.

Belle hesitated momentarily, then slowly nodded, her heart pounding with fear and vulnerability. With trembling hands, she fetched a small notepad and pen from her purse, scribbling down her most profound thoughts in delicate, flowing script.

"Ever since Jazz moved across the street, I've been longing to reconnect with him," Belle wrote, then handed the notepad to Maggie. "But I'm afraid of rejection - what if he doesn't feel the same way?"

Maggie read the words carefully, her eyes softening with understanding. She reached across the bench, enveloping Belle in a warm embrace. They sat like that for a moment, the comforting presence of their friendship helping to soothe Belle's fears.

"Love can be terrifying," Maggie admitted, pulling away slightly to look at Belle. "But no matter what happens, you still have a beautiful connection with Jazz. You owe it to yourself to explore those feelings and see where they lead you."

Belle took a deep breath, feeling the weight of Maggie's words settle in her heart. The fear was still there, but perhaps, just this once, she could find the courage to face it head-on. Love had always been worth fighting for; maybe it was time to retake that leap of faith.

The afternoon sun dappled the patio, casting warm, golden light on Belle and Maggie as they sat beneath the shade of a sprawling oak tree. A gentle breeze rustled through the leaves, carrying the faint scent of lilacs from the nearby garden. Belle's eyes shimmered with unspoken emotions, her fingers tracing the rim of her teacup as she searched for the right words.

"Sometimes, I feel this longing in my chest," Belle signed, her silver hair glinting in the sunlight. "I want to reach out to Jazz, but I'm scared."

Maggie leaned forward, her red curls brushing against her cheek as she listened intently. "It's never too late for love, Belle. You have so much history together; that connection is rare and precious."

Belle hesitated, her hands trembling ever so slightly as she signed, "What if we're too different after all these years?"

"Life has a way of changing us," Maggie replied gently. "But our hearts always remember where they belong. Don't let fear hold you back from pursuing happiness with Jazz."

As Maggie spoke, Belle felt a warmth bloom within her, chasing away the shadows of doubt that had clouded her heart. Her blue eyes met Maggie's, reflecting the determination that now filled her soul.

"You're right," Belle signed, the weight of her decision settling upon her shoulders. "I can't let fear dictate my choices. I must talk to Jazz and see if we still have a chance."

Maggie smiled, reaching over to squeeze Belle's hand reassuringly. "That's the spirit, dear friend. Whatever happens, know that you are brave for facing your fears, and you deserve every bit of happiness that comes your way."

Emboldened by Maggie's words, Belle felt a renewed hope coursing through her veins. She knew the road ahead would be fraught with uncertainty, but with a deep breath and unwavering resolve, she prepared to confront her past and embrace whatever future lay before her.

"Thank you, Maggie," Belle signed, her eyes shining with gratitude. "Your support means more than I can say."

"Always here for you, Belle," Maggie replied, her voice warm and tender. And as they looked into each other's eyes, they knew their friendship would remain a steadfast beacon of love and understanding no matter the outcome.

The golden sun dipped low in the sky, casting an ethereal glow over the porch where Jazz and Ray sat, their conversation peppered with the song of cicadas. The condensation on their lemonade glasses glistened as if holding onto the day's warmth.

"Jazz, my friend," Ray began, his voice gentle but firm. "I've learned through my experiences that forgiveness and second chances are crucial in any relationship. We all make mistakes and need to learn and grow from them."

Jazz nodded, his salt and pepper hair catching the last rays of sunlight. He knew Ray spoke from a place of truth, having lost his wife years ago and finding love again. His fingers traced the rim of the glass, contemplating the weight of Ray's words.

"Sometimes, we hold onto our fears so tightly that we miss out on the very thing we long for," Ray continued, his eyes searching Jazz's face for understanding. "Don't let the fear of getting hurt or disappointing Belle keep you from exploring this reconnection."

Jazz shifted in his seat, his tall frame betraying his vulnerability. "But how do I even approach her about this? Todd and Lynn have been so protective since we all connected."

"Find a way to talk to her alone, away from Todd and Lynn," Ray advised. "You both deserve a chance to express your true feelings without interference."

Jazz looked down at his hands, their veins etched like a roadmap of life lived and moments shared. He could feel the urgency of time slipping through his fingers, his diminishing eyesight a constant reminder of its relentless march.

"Life is too precious, Jazz," Ray said softly, touching his friend's shoulder. "Don't live with regrets. If there's even a chance that you and Belle can find happiness together again, you owe it to yourselves to try."

Jazz took a deep breath, inhaling the sweet scent of lilacs that wafted through the air. The memory of Belle's laughter danced in his mind, mingling with the distant chime of windchimes. He knew Ray was right; he couldn't let fear hold him back any longer.

"Thank you, Ray," Jazz murmured, his voice thick with emotion. "Your support means the world to me."

"Always here for you, my friend," Ray replied, his smile warm and genuine. As they sat in companionable silence, Jazz felt a newfound resolve taking root, fueled by the hope that a second chance at love might still be within reach.

Jazz stood up from the porch swing, determination coursing through his veins like a river in flood. He clapped Ray on the back, gratitude shining in his eyes.

"Thank you for everything, Ray," he said firmly. "You've given me the courage to face my fears and retake a chance on love."

Ray grinned, his eyes crinkling at the corners. "Go get her, Jazz. You know you two were meant to be together."

As Jazz took the first steps toward Belle's house, his heart fluttered like a sparrow in his chest, a mix of excitement and trepidation. His mind wandered back to their last dance, a tender waltz under a canopy of stars, with Belle's silver hair shimmering like moonlight. The memory was so vivid that it felt like he could reach out and touch her soft skin.

His mind wandered back to their last dance, a tender waltz under a canopy of stars, with Belle's hair shimmering like moonlight. Her gaze, filled with a depth of understanding that transcended words, had locked onto his, and for a moment, it was as if they were the only two people in the world. The memory was so vivid that it felt like he could reach out and touch her soft skin; the warmth of her hand in his still lingered.

Just as Jazz stepped onto the street, the loud sound of a car horn filled the air, shattering the moment's tranquility. Todd quickly pulled his father away from danger, guiding him back into the safety of their home. The door closed behind them with a soft thud, and Jazz leaned against the wall, catching his breath.

"Thanks, Todd," Jazz murmured, his heart racing from the near miss. "I guess I got a little lost in thought there."

"It's okay, Dad." Todd patted his father on the shoulder reassuringly. "Just promise me you'll be more careful."

Jazz nodded. "I promise." He hesitated for a moment before continuing. "And thank you, not just for this, but for everything you do for me. It means more than you know."

Todd's face softened; it wasn't often that his father expressed his emotions so openly. "Of course, Dad. I'm here for you no matter what."

Meanwhile, Belle sat at her kitchen table, her fingers absently tracing the worn edges of a photograph she had taken of Jazz years ago. Her expressive blue eyes clouded with emotion as they flicked between the smiling face in the picture and the empty chair beside her. She longed to feel Jazz's strong arms around her again, but fear held her captive like an invisible chain.

"Can I open myself up to love again?" she wondered silently. "Am I strong enough?"

A sudden gust of wind blew through the open window, ruffling the pages of her scrapbook and stirring a refreshing sense of anticipation within her. The breeze seemed to whisper its encouragement in response to her unspoken question. Belle straightened her back and clenched her fists, feeling the weight of her decision settling upon her shoulders like a cloak woven from hope and resolve.

Unbeknownst to each other, Jazz and Belle set their hearts on a collision course, each willing to take the leap and embrace the possibility of a renewed connection. Jazz felt his legs carry him toward her home again, moving as if propelled by an unseen force, while Belle gathered her treasured memories, preparing to lay them bare before the man who had once owned her heart.

"Jazz," she thought, "I'm ready."

Their paths merged just outside Belle's front door in the late night hours, as fate would have it. Startled, they stared at each other for a heartbeat, time standing still as they drank in the sight of one another.

"Hello, Belle," Jazz said softly, his voice trembling with emotion.

"Jazz," she signed, her eyes glistening with unshed tears.

At that moment, while their children were sleeping and the world was silent, they both understood that their hearts had been unknowingly entwined all along, waiting for the courage to rekindle a love that had never truly faded away. As they reached out to grasp each other's hands, the warmth of their connection seemed to chase away the shadows of fear and doubt, leaving only the promise of a brighter future together.

Jazz stood in his dimly lit living room, the soft glow of the setting sun casting a warm hue across the space. He glanced at the old wooden clock on the wall, its hands ticking steadily towards the hour. The anticipation of seeing Belle again swelled within him, bringing a flood of memories - their laughter echoing through the years, the delicate press of her lips against his, and how her eyes seemed to hold the entire world.

"Hey, Dad?" Todd's voice jolted Jazz from his reverie. "What's going on? You seem... different."

"Ah, Todd," Jazz replied, trying to keep his voice steady. "I was just thinking about Lynn and Belle and how long it's been since we've all talked. Maybe it's time for another visit, you know?"

"I agree, Dad." Todd hesitated before continuing. "Is there anything else you want to say?"

"Just thank you, Todd," Jazz said, touched by his son's understanding.

Meanwhile, at Belle's home, she sat in her cozy reading nook, pictures of her past with Jazz scattered around her like fallen leaves. Her heart fluttered as she traced the outline of Jazz's face in an old photograph, her fingers lingering on the creases that time had etched into his features.

"Mom, are you okay?" Lynn asked, her voice tinged with concern.

Belle looked up and smiled reassuringly, signing, "Yes, dear. Just feeling nostalgic."

"Is there anything I can do for you?" Lynn offered, her brow furrowed with worry.

"Actually," Belle signed, taking a deep breath, "I'd like to spend some time with Todd and Jazz. Can you arrange that?"

"Of course, Mom," Lynn replied, her eyes softening with understanding.

"Thank you, sweetheart. I want to make sure of some things with Todd," Belle signed, her heart swelling with gratitude.

As the day slipped into the evening, Jazz and Belle each found themselves consumed by thoughts of their upcoming visit. They had decided on a quiet spot near the river. Hopefully, Todd and Lynn would enjoy themselves and go for a long walk, which could probably lead to the possibility that Jazz and Belle could steal a kiss as they did as young lovers, away from prying eyes.

"Tomorrow, it is," Jazz muttered, his hands shaking as he dialed Belle's number to confirm the time and place.

"Hello?" came Lynn's voice on the other end.

"Hi, Lynn. This is Jazz. I hope we get to spend time with both of you tomorrow at the river. Could you let her know I will make the sandwiches?"

"Jazz," Lynn replied warmly. "I'll pass along the message."

"Thank you, Lynn," Jazz said before hanging up the phone, his heart racing with anticipation.

Having received Lynn's message, Belle felt excited as she imagined seeing Jazz again. She knew this was the moment she had been waiting for - the chance to confront their past and express the love that had never left her heart.

"Jazz," she signed to herself, her fingers dancing through the air like butterflies, "I'm ready."

Chapter 7

The sun dipped low in the sky, casting a warm golden glow over the river as Jazz and Belle walked along its banks. A gentle breeze rustled the leaves above them, filling the air with the sweet scent of blossoms. Jazz squinted into the distance, his salt and pepper hair ruffled by the wind. His eyesight had been failing him lately, coming and going like a finicky radio signal.

"Careful, Jazz," Belle warned, her eyes full of concern as she noticed him faltering on a protruding root. She reached out to steady him, her hand lightly resting on his arm.

"Thanks, Belle," he replied, flashing a grateful smile. "You're always looking out for me."

As they continued their walk, Jazz increasingly relied on Belle's steady presence for support. He took her arm, feeling the warmth of her skin against his own, and marveled at how seamlessly they moved together. Their footsteps were in sync, as though they'd been walking side by side for a lifetime.

"Jazz," Belle signed with her free hand, catching his attention. "Let's rest under that tree."

He followed her gaze to an old oak tree near the water's edge, its branches reaching out like welcoming arms. As they settled down beneath its comforting shade, the world seemed to fade away, leaving only the two within its embrace.

"Beautiful spot, isn't it?" Jazz mused, admiring the way the sunlight danced on the rippling water.

Belle nodded and turned to face him, her blue eyes shining with emotion. Jazz could see the love and longing that had remained unspoken for decades in those depths. The intensity of her gaze struck him, the way it seemed to pierce right through him as if she was trying to communicate something beyond words.

"Jazz," she signed again, her hands trembling slightly. "I need you to know..."

But words were not enough for Belle; she needed Jazz to feel her love, to experience it in a way that transcended language. Her eyes never leaving him, she leaned in and pressed her lips against his. It was their first kiss in over fifty years, but it felt like coming home.

Jazz was now momentarily taken aback by the unexpected tenderness of the moment. He hesitated but then wrapped his arms around Belle, pulling her close as they deepened the kiss. All the years of separation melted away, and together, they rediscovered the passionate connection that had once burned so brightly between them.

As they finally broke apart, breathless and flushed, Jazz couldn't help but smile at Belle's radiant expression. He knew that their lives had changed irrevocably, their hearts forever intertwined.

"Thank you, Belle," he whispered, his voice thick with emotion. "I don't have the words to tell you how much this means to me."

"Words don't always matter," she signed back, eyes full of love and understanding. "Sometimes all we need is to be truly seen and held by someone."

And beneath the ancient oak tree, Jazz and Belle held each other, finding solace and strength in one another's embrace. Love had found its way of speaking, loud and clear, without a single word.

As the sun dipped below the horizon, casting a warm golden glow over the riverbank, Belle reached for Jazz's hand. Her fingers intertwined with his, creating a perfect fit that felt familiar and new. The gentle pressure of her touch conveyed a thousand unspoken words of love and support, filling the spaces between them where words could not reach.

"Feels just like it did all those years ago," Jazz murmured, his voice tinged with wonder as he squeezed her hand gently.

Belle smiled at him, her eyes sparkling affectionately, and nodded in agreement. She then moved her free hand to rest on his shoulder, offering him additional stability as they continued their leisurely walk along the river. Jazz could feel the warmth of her palm seeping through the fabric of his shirt, spreading comfort and reassurance throughout his body.

"Sometimes I think I rely on you too much," Jazz confessed, battling the mixed emotions of gratitude and guilt that threatened to overwhelm him.

In response, Belle shook her head, her unwavering gaze never leaving his face. She tightened her grip on his hand and brought it up to her heart, letting him feel its steady rhythm. Jazz understood; she wanted him to know that he wasn't a burden but a cherished part of her life that she wouldn't trade for anything. It was a sentiment that resonated deep within him, and he felt tears prickling at the corners of his eyes.

"Thank you, Belle," he said softly. "I don't know what I'd do without you."

She smiled, her eyes full of tenderness, and leaned against his shoulder as they walked.

As the days passed, their connection grew more substantial, with Belle consistently finding new ways to communicate her love through touch. Whether resting a hand on Jazz's back as they stood side by side or tracing her fingers along the lines of his palm, each gesture served as a powerful reminder of the bond they shared. It was an unspoken language that grew richer and more intimate with time.

Jazz relied on Belle's touch as a source of comfort and reassurance, particularly when his eyesight waned, leaving him adrift in a world of shadows and blurred shapes. No matter how dark or uncertain things became, Belle's presence remained a beacon of light, guiding him through life's hardships and challenges.

"Promise me one thing," Jazz whispered one night as they lay under the stars, their hands clasped together. "Promise me that we'll always have each other no matter what happens."

"I promise," Belle signed, her fingers dancing gracefully through the air. Her hand then returned to his, giving it a firm squeeze.

They both knew there would be a better time to let Todd and Lynn know about their history, but for now, they reveled in the simple joy of reuniting quietly. Together, they faced the world hand in hand, their love transcending the boundaries of spoken language and the limitations of mortal bodies. Ultimately, love was all they needed, and it was more substantial than anything that life could throw at them.

Jazz's vision blurred and steadied as he squinted at the soft light reflecting off the river. Belle, perceptive as always, seemed to sense his struggle and moved closer to him, her shoulder brushing against his arm. Even without words, she understood him better than anyone else ever had.

"Thank you," Jazz murmured, allowing himself a moment to lean on her for support. His voice was barely audible, even to himself, but he knew she'd understand.

Belle smiled warmly in response, her blue eyes shining with love and tenderness. The corners of her eyes crinkled as her smile spread across her face, a testament to the joy that bubbled beneath their shared connection.

Feeling her gaze on him, Jazz did his best to return the gesture, offering a lopsided grin despite his unreliable eyesight. In those moments when his vision failed him, Jazz found solace in the warmth of Belle's hand as it gently found his fingers intertwining effortlessly.

"Your hands are so warm," Jazz said, his voice slightly shaky. "I can feel your love through them."

Her cheeks flushed a lovely shade of pink, and Belle squeezed his hand in affirmation. Jazz could see the sincerity in her eyes, even as everything around them became a hazy blur.

"Every touch, every smile, they mean more to me than any words ever could," he confessed, his heart swelling with emotion. "You're my compass, Belle. You guide me through the darkness."

Her eyes filled with tears at his heartfelt confession, and Belle leaned in closer, placing her free hand on his cheek. She allowed her thumb to trace the lines of his face gently, and Jazz closed his eyes, savoring the intimate connection between them.

"Sometimes I wish I could see you clearer, Belle. But even when I can't, I know you're there, and that's enough for me," Jazz whispered, his voice thick with emotion.

Belle nodded, her eyes never leaving his face. The world seemed to disappear around them as they stood by the river, their love transcending spoken language and physical limitations. There was a beauty in their silent communication, something unspoken yet powerful.

"Jazz," Belle signed after quiet contemplation, her eyes shining with determination. "I'm here, and I always will be."

"Thank you, Belle," Jazz said, his voice barely more than a whisper. "Thank you for being my light."

Together, they stood by the water's edge, hands clasped tightly, hearts entwined. Despite the challenges life threw at them, they found solace and strength in each other's presence, their love expressed in smiles, touches, and unwavering devotion.

The shadows of the trees danced on the ground as the sun dipped lower in the sky, casting a warm golden glow upon Jazz and Belle. Sitting quietly side by side, they leaned against an old oak tree trunk, their hands gently clasped together. The river flowed nearby, its gentle murmurs providing a soothing soundtrack for their secret rendezvous.

"Jazz," Belle signed, her fingers moving gracefully through the air, "do you remember the day we first met?"

"Of course," he responded, his voice soft and dreamy. "It was at the county fair all those years ago. You wore that yellow dress with white polka dots, and your hair was tied up in ribbons. I didn't think you even noticed me."

Jazz could still picture how Belle looked that day despite his fading vision. It seemed as though time had only added to her beauty, her silver hair shining like moonlight and her eyes brimming with love and wisdom. He smiled at the memory, squeezing her hand gently in reassurance.

"Your laughter was like music to my ears," he continued. "I knew from that moment that you were someone special."

Belle blushed, her cheeks turning a soft pink. She leaned closer to Jazz, resting her head on his shoulder as they shared the warmth of their memories.

Over time, their secret meetings by the river had become a cherished routine, an opportunity to escape the world and bask in the comfort of each other's presence. Words often felt unnecessary, as they communicated through touch and the emotions that shone brightly in their eyes.

One day, as Jazz returned home from a walk, he found a small envelope waiting for him on his porch. Upon recognizing Belle's elegant handwriting on the front, his heart warmed. Carefully, he unfolded the note inside, tracing his fingers over her words:

"Jazz, my love,

Our time together is more precious than gold,

A sanctuary where our hearts grow young and bold.

Forever, I will cherish these moments we share,

Our love unspoken, yet felt in the air."

Though his vision blurred the letters, Jazz could feel the depth of Belle's emotions emanating from the page. He carried her words close to his heart, tucked safely within his worn leather jacket pocket.

In return, Belle surprised Jazz with small acts of kindness, from preparing his favorite meal – a hearty beef stew – to ensuring his garden was always filled with blooming flowers, their colors bright enough to appreciate even with his failing eyesight.

These gestures spoke louder than words ever could, a testament to their unwavering bond and the language of love they had created together. And so, beneath the shade of the old oak tree, they continued to hold hands, sharing the gift of each other's presence as the sun set and the stars began to twinkle in the twilight sky.

Jazz sat on the porch, the sun casting warm rays on his face as he listened to the distant chirping of birds. A soft smile graced his lips; he had a plan – a surprise for Belle and Lynn. He knew just how much they loved art, and there was a new exhibit at the local museum. The thought of spending an afternoon together and sharing their interests made him feel closer to them.

"Ready to go, Jazz?" Todd asked, snapping Jazz out of his reverie.

"Ah, yes," Jazz replied, standing and adjusting his hat. "It's going to be a lovely day."

As they approached Belle's home, Jazz felt a flutter of excitement. Belle stepped outside, her blue eyes bright with anticipation, while Lynn followed close behind, a soft smile playing on her lips.

"Good morning, Jazz," Belle signed, her hands moving gracefully through the air. "What do you have planned for today?"

"Morning, Belle," Jazz responded, enjoying the sight of her silver hair catching the sunlight. "I thought we could all visit the art museum today. I heard there's a wonderful new exhibit."

Belle's eyes lit up, and Lynn said, "That sounds perfect Jazz. Mom and I have been wanting to see it."

As they strolled toward the museum and beyond the eyesight of Todd and Lynn, Jazz reached for Belle's hand, feeling the warmth of her fingers intertwining with his own. He didn't need words to tell her how much she meant to him; their connection went beyond language, residing within their hearts.

Inside the museum, they wandered through the halls, admiring the artwork and sharing stories from their past. Jazz reveled in Belle's laughter, a melody that resonated deeply within him.

"Did I ever tell you about when I accidentally painted my dog?" Lynn chuckled, recalling the memory. "I was working on a piece and left my paint out, and well... let's just say he became a walking masterpiece."

"Ah, yes," Jazz responded, his eyes crinkling with amusement.

They continued exploring the exhibit, occasionally stopping at a particular painting or sculpture that caught their eye. Jazz would sometimes guide Belle to a breathtaking piece, describing it in vivid detail so she could envision it through his words.

"Imagine a sunset over the ocean, Belle," Jazz whispered tenderly as they stood before a magnificent landscape. "The sky a brilliant canvas of oranges, reds, and purples, reflecting upon the water like an artist's dream."

Belle's eyes closed, her hand gripping Jazz's tighter as she savored the image painted within her mind.

"Thank you, Jazz," she signed, her eyes soft with appreciation.

"Anything for you, Belle," he replied, his heart swelling with love for her.

As they departed the museum, their hands still joined, Jazz couldn't help but think about how their time together had become a sanctuary – a place where their hearts found solace in one another. They no longer needed words to convey their love; their story, rich with memories and laughter, was a testament to their unbreakable bond.

And as the sun descended, casting a golden glow upon their intertwined fingers, Jazz knew he would cherish these moments forever – their silent symphony of love, transcending language and time.

The sun dipped low, casting a warm glow on the porch where Belle and Jazz sat together, a muted symphony of crickets serenading them in the early evening. Belle's silver hair caught the light, shimmering like a halo as she leaned over a small notebook, her pen dancing gracefully across the page. Jazz observed her with a tender smile, his salt and pepper hair ruffling slightly in the breeze.

"Jazz, I've been thinking," Belle signed with one hand while holding her pen, "I want to communicate my love for you through words as well." She tapped the notebook gently.

"Words from your heart," Jazz replied softly, leaning in to read the delicate script on the page. Despite the fading light and his unwelcome reliance on touch more than sight, he could make out a few lines of poetry:

"Time may wither, eyes may fade,

But our love, a dance, is unchanged.

In silence, whispers undeterred,

Our hearts entwined, forever heard."

A profound emotion swelled within him, threatening to spill over as tears. He grasped Belle's free hand,
bringing it to his lips for a gentle kiss. "Thank you,
Belle. Your words mean everything to me."

"Let me teach you and Todd sign language, too, so we
can all communicate better," Belle proposed, her blue
eyes sparkling with determination.

"Teach me now," Jazz requested earnestly, eager to
learn this new language of love.

Belle placed her pen down and began instructing
Jazz, their hands intertwining and dancing in the air as
she taught him the signs for 'I love you,' 'happiness,'
and 'forever.' The warmth of her touch, the way her
fingers guided his, created an intimate connection that
reached beyond words.

"Will you teach this to Todd as well?" Jazz asked after
they had practiced several signs together.

"Of course," Belle nodded, her smile lighting up her
face. "We're all family."

As the days passed, Jazz and Todd learned sign language
from Belle, their bond deepening as they embraced this
new form of communication. And every so often, Belle
would leave a handwritten note for Jazz, each message a
tender expression of her love. Even with his diminishing

eyesight, Jazz would trace the words with his fingertips, feeling the depth of her emotions through the ink.

"Another note from Belle?" Todd asked one day, noticing his father's gentle smile as he held a piece of paper close to his heart.

"Yes," Jazz sighed contentedly, running his fingers over the words one last time before tucking the note safely into his pocket. "Her words are like a lifeline, connecting our hearts even apart."

"Something special is happening for the Montgomery men, Dad," Todd remarked, his voice thick with emotion. "I think so."

"I hope so, son," Jazz replied, his hand reaching his pocket, where the precious notes rested against his heart. "I hope so."

A warm breeze rustled the leaves overhead as Jazz and Belle sat side by side on a worn wooden bench overlooking the river. The sun cast dappled shadows on the ground, its rays filtering through the swaying branches above them. Jazz felt the warmth of Belle's presence beside him, her slender hand resting gently on his thigh.

"Such a beautiful day," Jazz murmured, turning towards Belle with a heartfelt smile. He squinted, trying to make out the familiar lines of her face, but all he could see was a blur of silver hair and vibrant blue eyes.

Belle nodded, her gaze never leaving Jazz's face. She reached up and tenderly brushed his cheek with the back of her hand, tracing the curve of his jawline. Her touch spoke volumes, conveying her love for him, but she couldn't express it.

"Even if I can't see it all clearly, I feel it," Jazz said softly, placing his hand over hers. "I feel your love, Belle."

"Love" – she signed the word, moving her hands gracefully in front of her chest. Jazz mirrored the movement, grateful for the shared language they were building together.

"Love," he repeated, then added with a chuckle, "You know, it'd be easier if I could just sign 'I love you too,' but we'll get there."

Belle smiled, her eyes shining affectionately, and patted his hand reassuringly. She then took his other hand and intertwined their fingers, using touch to strengthen their connection.

"Thank you for teaching me and Todd, Belle," Jazz said, his voice filled with gratitude. "It means so much to us both."

"Family," – Belle signed, her expression full of warmth and sincerity.

"Family," – Jazz echoed, feeling a surge of emotion inside him. As they sat there, hands clasped together, he realized that their love transcended words and the limitations of his eyesight. They had forged a bond that was stronger than any physical barrier.

"May I?" Jazz asked hesitantly, leaning in towards Belle. She nodded, her eyes filled with anticipation. He closed the distance between them, feeling the warmth of her breath on his face as he gently pressed his lips against hers.

The kiss was tender and sweet, reaffirming their love for each other after so many years apart. As they pulled away, Jazz rested his forehead against Belle's, reveling in the moment's intimacy.

"Thank you," he whispered, his voice thick with emotion. "Thank you for never giving up on us."

"Always," – Belle signed, her fingers brushing against his cheek.

"Always," – Jazz repeated, pulling her into a tight embrace. Their hearts overflowed with love and gratitude for one another, bound by a connection that would never be broken.

The sun shone warmly through the ice cream shop's window, bathing Jazz and Todd in golden light as they sat at their favorite corner booth. The clink of spoons and the laughter of families filled the air, creating an atmosphere of contentment.

"Remember how we used to come here after your soccer games?" Jazz said, reminiscing with a nostalgic glint in his eyes. "You always ordered mint chocolate chip without fail."

Todd chuckled, his eyes softening. "Yeah, I remember. And you'd get that rum raisin flavor no one else liked."

"Ah, yes, the misunderstood treasure," Jazz joked, leaning back into the booth with a pleased sigh. "Those were good times, weren't they?"

"Definitely," Todd agreed, his voice gentle as he reached over to pat his father's hand. The simple touch conveyed a warmth that words often failed to express.

"Excuse me? Can I take your order?" A cheerful voice interrupted their conversation, and they placed their orders: mint chocolate chip for Todd and rum raisin for Jazz.

Jazz listened intently to the sounds around him as they waited for their treats, attempting to paint a picture of their surroundings in his mind's eye. The door chime jingled, announcing a new customer's arrival, but Jazz paid little attention, lost in his thoughts.

"Hey, Lynn, what are you doing here?" Todd asked, surprised as he spotted her entering the shop.

"Mom and I were just out shopping. Thought I'd treat her to some ice cream," Lynn replied, her eyes sparkling warmly. She glanced at the newcomer who had entered behind her, her expression suddenly tense. "Oh, hey... Ryan."

"Long time no see, Lynn," Ryan said, his voice strained but polite. Jazz instantly sensed a shift in the atmosphere, feeling the tension seep into the air.

"Ryan? As in... your ex-boyfriend Ryan?" Todd asked cautiously, concern etched into his features.

"Yeah," Lynn sighed, her voice wavering slightly. "I didn't expect to run into him here."

"Neither did I," Ryan admitted, awkwardly rubbing the back of his neck. But it's nice to see you again, Lynn." He glanced at Jazz and Todd, offering them a tight-lipped smile. "Hello, sir. You must be Jazz and Todd Montgomery, right?"

"Indeed, we are," Jazz replied, forcing a warm smile onto his face despite his uneasiness. "And you're Ryan, I presume?"

"Yep, that's me," Ryan confirmed, shifting from foot to foot as he navigated the unexpected encounter. "I've heard a lot about you, sir. Lynn always spoke very highly of you."

"Thank you, son. That's kind of you to say," Jazz responded, his tone gracious but guarded.

"Hey, why don't we all sit together?" Todd suggested, attempting to dispel the tension. "There's no reason we can't be civil, right?"

"Sounds good to me," Ryan agreed hesitantly, taking a seat across from Jazz. As the group settled into an uneasy camaraderie, Jazz couldn't help but wonder how this chance encounter would affect their delicate balance of love and family.

Chapter 8

The television in Mrs. Davis' Ice Cream Shop flickered with static as the weather report echoed through the small, crowded space. Jazz Montgomery squinted his failing eyes at the screen, trying to decipher the images of strong winds, pouring rain, and flashes of lightning. The once joyful gathering had turned uncomfortable as Lynn's ex-boyfriend, Ryan, had shown up unexpectedly. Belle Thompson's expressive blue eyes filled with unease, her stillness betraying her distress.

"Looks like there's a storm coming," Jazz said softly, his voice imbued with nostalgia. He could feel the tension rising in the room, the air thick with unspoken words.

"Mom, we should get going," Lynn suggested. Her gentle touch on her mother's arm showed her concern for Belle. She glanced at Ryan, who seemed aware of his effect on Belle.

"All right," Belle nodded, her gaze locking onto Jazz for a moment before she turned toward the door.

As they prepared to leave, Lynn stepped closer to Ryan, her warm smile replaced by a severe expression. "Ryan, I'm asking you, please don't let this happen again. Your presence upsets Mom."

"Okay, Lynn," Ryan replied, understanding in his eyes. "I just wanted to see her again, but I know how much she means to you."

"Thank you," Lynn whispered, relief washing over her face as she followed Jazz and her mother into the stormy night.

"Let's head to my place," Todd offered, leading the way to his home.

"Good idea, son," Jazz agreed, sensing the need for shelter from the storm and the emotional turbulence surrounding them all.

They entered Todd's basement, a cozy space filled with books and comfortable furniture. Todd busied himself lighting candles, their flames casting flickering shadows on the walls. Jazz, Belle, and Lynn settled in, the weight of the day catching up with them.

"Storms like these always bring memories," Jazz said wistfully as he looked at Belle. He could see the anxiety in her eyes, mirroring his own as they both thought back to that fateful night fifty years ago when their lives had taken different paths.

"Mom has always had a thing about storms," Lynn mentioned, her voice soft and thoughtful. "She says they remind her of the beauty in chaos."

"Your mom's a wise woman," Jazz replied, smiling at Belle.

As the storm raged outside, the unlikely group found solace in each other's presence, the flickering candlelight casting a warm glow over their faces. They huddled together, seeking comfort amid the chaos, united by a shared history that stretched far beyond what they had realized.

Rain lashed against the basement windows, the howling wind punctuated by the occasional crack of thunder. Jazz gazed at the rivulets streaking down the glass, his eyesight blurred and strained. The storm's ferocity seemed to mirror the turmoil he felt inside.

"Wow, look at those branches," Todd said, peering out the window. "They're practically horizontal."

"It seems like the whole town is getting hit hard," Lynn chimed in, her voice a mix of concern and awe. She stared at the water pooling in the streets and the chaotic dance of debris caught in the torrent.

Jazz glanced at Belle, noting the worry in the lines around her eyes. He reached for her hand, giving it a reassuring squeeze. "I remember a storm like this fifty years ago," he said, his voice barely audible above the din outside. Each word felt heavy, weighed down by the memories they carried.

Belle looked at him, her blue eyes wide and filled with emotion. She nodded slowly as if to say she remembered, too. The storm had stirred up more than just the wind and rain; it had unearthed a shared past buried under the sands of time.

"Is everything okay?" Todd asked, sensing the tension between his father and Belle.

"Of course," Jazz replied, forcing a smile. "Just reminiscing about old times."

"Storms can bring back memories," Lynn said softly, her gaze fixed on her mother. "Both good and bad."

As the storm continued its relentless assault, Jazz couldn't help but think back to that fateful night when he and Belle had lost touch. It seemed like a lifetime ago, yet the pain lingered, sharp and raw.

"Hey, Dad?" Todd's voice cut through Jazz's reverie. "Do you want to share some of those memories with us?"

Jazz hesitated, the words caught in his throat. He glanced at Belle, her eyes pleading for understanding. "Maybe another time," he said finally, knowing that some stories were better left untold.

"Sure thing," Todd replied, nodding respectfully. "Some things are meant to be cherished privately."

The four of them sat silently, listening to the storm as it battered the town outside. Each was lost in their thoughts yet bound together by a growing sense of connection and understanding.

As the wind howled and the rain fell, Jazz held onto Belle's hand – a lifeline tethering him to the present. And in that moment, amidst the chaos and unease, they found solace in each other's embrace, weathering the storm together.

The flickering candlelight cast a warm glow across the four faces huddled together in Todd's basement, chasing away the shadows that lurked in the corners. The wind howled like a wounded animal outside, its rage rattling the windows as if it were desperate to get in. But inside, there was warmth and comfort, a sanctuary from the storm.

"Here," Jazz murmured, draping an arm around Belle's shoulders, drawing her close. "We'll keep each other warm."

Todd and Lynn exchanged glances, surprise and curiosity mingling as they saw their parents embracing. It was a tender moment that seemed to hint at a shared history between Jazz and Belle—a record their children had never been privy to.

"Is everyone all right?" Todd asked, his voice barely audible above the din of the storm. He shifted closer to his father and Belle, wrapping his arm around Lynn.

"Y-yes," Lynn stammered, her teeth chattering from the chill in the air. "It's just so c-cold."

"Here," Jazz said softly, pulling Todd and Lynn into the embrace. "We're all warmer together."

As the rain hammered against the windows, the four of them huddled even closer, seeking solace in the warmth and comfort of each other's presence. Jazz could feel Belle's heartbeat against his chest, steady and robust, a testament to the resilience she had always possessed. He knew she must remember that stormy night fifty years ago – when everything had changed for them.

"Mom," Lynn whispered, her voice shaking with emotion. "Are you okay?"

Belle looked up at her daughter, her expressive blue eyes glistening with unshed tears. She nodded slowly, squeezing Lynn's hand reassuringly.

"Storms can be frightening," Jazz said gently and understandingly. "But they also have a way of bringing people together."

"Like tonight," Todd added, giving his father a small smile. "If it weren't for this storm, we wouldn't all be here, huddled together like this."

"Right," Jazz agreed, nodding. Sometimes, the things that scare us can also help us grow stronger and forge deeper connections with the ones we love."

As the storm continued to rage outside—its fury a stark contrast to the warmth and closeness they shared in the basement—Jazz couldn't help but wonder what the future held for them. The past might have been filled with heartache and regret, but there was still hope for healing, for finding solace and strength in the embrace of those who truly understood.

They were now united in their vulnerability, bound by the power of a shared experience. As the rain continued to pour down, washing away the remnants of the past, it seemed as if a new sense of love was being born from the chaos – a love that would withstand even the fiercest storms.

The flickering candlelight cast a warm glow over their faces as raindrops drummed against the windows. Jazz's mind wandered, the storm's intensity stirring up memories from long ago. He could almost see himself in the pouring rain, drenched and heartbroken.

"Storms always make me think of one night long ago," Jazz said softly, his voice barely audible above the wind's howl. "I was caught in the rain, feeling lost and alone. That night changed my life forever." He did not mention Belle, but she seemed to understand, her eyes glistening with unshed tears.

Todd and Lynn exchanged a glance, sensing there was more to the story. Todd cleared his throat, attempting to lighten the mood. "You know, storms have played a big part in our lives, too," he began, a slight tremor in his voice betraying his unease.

Lynn nodded, gently squeezing her mother's hand. "Yeah, a huge storm hit our town when I was little. We lost power for days, and it scared me so much that I stayed glued to Mom's side. But as we lit candles and read stories together, I realized there was a comfort to be found even in the darkest moments."

"Same here," Todd chimed in. "As a teenager, I got caught in a downpour during a hike with Dad. It was terrifying, but it forced us to work together to rely on each other. That experience brought us closer than ever before."

As they shared their stories, their connection grew more pungent, solidified by their shared experience of finding solace amidst the storm. Jazz's gaze met Belle's, and though they did not speak, their eyes conveyed a depth of understanding that no words could match.

"Life is full of storms," Jazz mused, watching the rain streak the windowpanes. "But how we weather them, grow from the chaos, and find strength in each other truly matters."

"Exactly," Lynn agreed, her voice filled with a newfound conviction. "Together, we can face whatever storms come our way."

Their hearts intertwined. They sat in silent communion, warmed by the candlelight and each other's presence, as the storm outside roared on.

The storm's howl intensified, drowning out the pattering of rain against the windows. The flickering candlelight cast shadows that danced along the walls of Todd's basement, mirroring the stormy turmoil outside. As the four sat huddled together in an attempt to find solace in the chaos, the silvery strands of Belle's hair caught Jazz's attention. Their eyes met, and time seemed to stand still for a moment.

Silence enveloped the room, broken only by the hushed breaths of those gathered within. And then, as if carried by the wind, Belle whispered words she had never been able to say. "I never stopped loving you," her voice barely audible yet pierced through the storm's din. "Even after fifty years, I still love you."

Jazz felt his heart constrict, the weight of the words settling deep within him. He could see the emotions swimming behind Belle's blue eyes – a mixture of hope, longing, and vulnerability – as she held his gaze. It took all his strength not to reach out and pull her into his arms; instead, he let the warmth of her confession wash over him.

Todd and Lynn exchanged confused glances before turning their questioning eyes toward their respective parents. Neither had known about the connection between Jazz and Belle, and the revelation left them reeling. "Wait, you two knew each other before we moved across the street?" Lynn asked, her words laced with disbelief.

"Jazz and I were close friends when we were young," Belle explained, her voice still shaky from her previous declaration. "We lost touch during a storm much like this one. Life took us down different paths, but our hearts never strayed far from each other."

Nostalgia filled Jazz's chest, mingling with the regret that had haunted him for decades. But now, as they sat together, the storm raging outside, he felt a spark of resilience ignite. "We can't change the past, but we're here now," he said softly, his eyes never leaving Belle's. "And this time, we'll weather the storm together."

Belle nodded, her silver hair catching the flickering candlelight once more. The raw vulnerability in her eyes was replaced by determination and hope, reflecting Jazz's resolve.

As the storm continued to batter the town outside, the four huddled closer, each finding solace in the other's warmth and presence. Amid chaos and uncertainty, they discovered a newfound connection forged by a love that had endured for half a century. And as the winds howled and rain poured down, Jazz knew they were strong enough to withstand any storm life might throw their way together.

The rain outside began to calm, its once violent patter against the windows now a gentle and soothing murmur. The candlelight flickered softly across their faces, casting shadows that danced and swayed with the shifting flame. They sat in the dimly lit basement, finding solace in the shared experience of vulnerability and the unshakeable bond that had formed between them.

"Remember when we were kids, and we'd hide under the covers during storms like this?" Jazz asked, his voice nostalgic as he gazed at Belle. "We thought we were invincible back then."

Belle smiled warmly, her blue eyes shining with the memories of their youth. She nodded, her hands gently clasping his. "I remember," she whispered, her voice barely audible above the rain's steady rhythm. "We were fearless."

Lynn looked from her mother to Jazz, her eyes searching for a connection to this past she knew nothing about. Todd, too, was deep in thought, trying to reconcile the new information about his father with the man he had known all his life.

"Mom, how come you never told me about Jazz?" Lynn ventured, her voice hesitant but full of curiosity.

Belle sighed, her gaze drifting towards the window as if the answer lay within the raindrops. "It was a part of my past I thought I'd left behind. But now I see that it was always meant to be a part of our present."

"And ours too, it seems," Todd added quietly, his reserved personality softening as he allowed himself to accept the turn of events. "Dad, what happened between you and Belle? Why did you lose touch?"

Jazz took a deep breath, the weight of years of silence lifting from his shoulders as he prepared to share his story. "It was a storm like this one fifty years ago. We were supposed to meet up, but the weather had other plans. We were separated, and life took us down different paths."

"Until now," Belle interjected softly, her hand reassuringly squeezing Jazz.

"Yes, until now," Jazz confirmed, his voice full of gratitude for the second chance they'd been given.

The basement fell into a moment of quiet reflection as each pondered the significance of the storm outside and its impact on their lives. In that shared silence, a deeper understanding of one another emerged, and they marveled at the resilience of love that had endured through time and distance.

"Life sure has a funny way of bringing people together, doesn't it?" Lynn mused, breaking the silence with a small smile.

"Indeed, it does," Jazz agreed, his eyes meeting Belle's once more. "And I wouldn't have it any other way."

As the storm began to subside, its chaos replaced by a newfound sense of connection, they knew they would face whatever lay ahead. And with that knowledge came the promise of a love that could weather any storm.

The last droplets of rain fell softly outside, casting a soothing pitter-patter against the small basement window. Four figures sat huddled together, their shadows cast upon the walls by the flickering candlelight. The storm had raged and howled for hours, but now, in its wake, an atmosphere of warmth and connection lingered.

Todd looked around at the faces of his father, Jazz, Belle, and Lynn, all shadowed by the dim light but illuminated by the raw emotions they'd shared throughout the night. He cleared his throat, breaking the silence in the room. "This was something tonight," he said softly, shaking his head in disbelief.

Lynn turned to face her mother, her eyes wide with amazement. "I had no idea that you two knew each other," she whispered, her gaze shifting between Belle and Jazz. "And the fact that it was about love..." Her voice trailed off, leaving the words to hang in the air like the scent of the extinguished candles.

Belle's blue eyes shimmered, reflecting the flickering light from the remaining candles. She gave a faint nod, acknowledging her daughter's surprise, and reached out a hand to touch Jazz's arm gently. His weathered face softened as he leaned into her touch, a sense of peace washing over him.

"Love is a powerful thing," Jazz murmured, his voice filled with a lifetime of memories and regret. "It can survive even the fiercest storms and the longest separations."

Todd watched his father, struck by the vulnerability he displayed. It was a rare moment when Jazz allowed himself to be open, and Todd couldn't help but feel moved by the resilience of the love between his father and Belle. A warmth bloomed within him, spreading through his chest like tendrils of ivy reaching toward the sun.

As the four of them sat there, sharing in the intimacy of the dimly lit basement, they found solace in the knowledge that the storm had brought them closer together and rekindled a love thought lost to time. The echoes of the past mingled with the present, creating a bridge between the two that could withstand the weight of their collective memories and emotions.

"Life is full of surprises," Lynn said quietly, her eyes filled with wonder as she looked at her mother and Jazz. "And sometimes, the most unexpected moments are the ones that bring us the greatest happiness."

"Indeed," Jazz agreed, his voice thick with emotion. "Even after all these years, it's still true."

In the aftermath of the storm, the basement had become a sanctuary for the four of them, where old wounds were laid bare and new bonds forged. As the last candle flickered out, leaving them bathed in darkness, they knew the storm raging outside had forever changed their lives. And within that darkness, a new sense of love had taken root, one that would guide them through the uncertainties of life and provide shelter from the storms yet to come.

Chapter 9

J azz and Belle sat in comfortable silence in Todd's cozy
living room. Fading sunlight filtered through the curtains, glowing warmly on their intertwined hands. Belle's
beautiful blue eyes shimmered with unspoken emotions,
and exhaustion was evident on her delicate features. With a
tender smile, she raised her free hand and gracefully signed,
"I'm a little tired."

Jazz leaned in closer, his salt and pepper hair catching
the light, and chuckled softly. "You know, for a moment
there, I thought you made my eyesight better," he said, his
voice laden with affection. "I was shocked when I heard

your voice, but I haven't been that happy to hear someone in a long time."

Belle's face lit up, her silver hair framing her expressive eyes. Their love and understanding transcended words like two souls entwined by fate. Jazz's heart swelled, and he felt a vulnerability he hadn't experienced in years. Gently pulling Belle into an embrace, he could feel the warmth of her body against his, a testament to the depth of their connection.

"Your voice brought me back in time," Jazz continued a mere whisper against Belle's ear. "Back when we were young, you told me how much you loved me. It reminded me of the angel who was placed in my life all those years ago."

As Belle's eyes brimmed with tears, her loving gaze locked onto Jazz's. In that instant, they both knew their bond had only grown stronger.

The door to the living room creaked open, and Jazz felt a sudden cool breeze against his warm cheek. Todd entered with Lynn by his side, their eyes wide with astonishment as they took in the tender scene before them.

"Mom?" Lynn's voice trembled with surprise, her gaze never leaving Belle's face. "That was you speaking?"

Belle looked up at her daughter, her blue eyes shining like sapphires. She gave a gentle nod, knowing how much this moment meant to both of them. As she opened her mouth to speak again, her voice came out as a whisper, barely audible but unmistakably hers. "Yes, my dear."

Todd marveled at the sound of Belle's voice, curiosity and amazement etched on his strong-jawed face. He glanced at his father, who was still holding Belle tightly and saw the tears glistening in Jazz's eyes.

The sunlight streamed through the kitchen window, casting a warm glow on Belle's silver hair. As she made her way to the counter, her gnarled fingers worked gracefully as she prepared breakfast. The aroma of freshly brewed coffee and homemade pancakes filled the air, enveloping Lynn in a familiar sense of comfort.

"Mom," Lynn said, taking a step closer, her long blonde hair falling over her shoulders. "I can't believe I'm hearing your voice again. It reminds me of the pureness of your heart, and it's like you're teaching me about love all over again."

Belle looked into her daughter's eyes, those same expressive blue orbs that mirrored her own. Though no words left her lips, her gaze spoke volumes. Her hands danced in the air, fingers shaping sentences as effortlessly as a painter's brush on canvas. Lynn watched intently, feeling the weight of every unspoken word resonate within her.

"Thank you, sweetheart," Belle replied, her chest swelling with pride for her daughter. Lynn embodied everything Belle had ever hoped for—how she carried herself and her exuded strength.

Lynn's eyes brimmed with tears, and she felt overwhelming gratitude for her mother's unwavering support and guidance. As she stood there, basking in the warmth of their connection, she couldn't help but reflect on the countless times Belle had been there for her. From skinned knees to broken hearts, her mother had been a constant source of solace and wisdom.

"Mom, how did you do it?" Lynn asked, her voice trembling. "How did you always find a way to bring love into our lives, even when it seemed impossible?"

Belle paused, her fingers intertwined as if searching for the right words. Her eyes soften as she thinks about the framed photographs lining the walls of their home. Images of family vacations, birthdays, and cherished moments adorned the wooden frames, each a testament to the love that had shaped their lives.

"Love is everywhere, my darling," Belle's hands conveyed. "You just have to be open to it."

Lynn felt her heart swell with appreciation for her mother's silent wisdom. At that moment, she understood that love could still be found in the most unexpected places, even when words were absent.

Lynn's gaze drifted to the sunlight streaming through the window. The love she felt in that moment seemed almost too much to bear, stirring memories of her father, Albert, who had been gone for years. She blinked back tears as she struggled to understand how such love could still burn so brightly despite the passage of time.

"Mom," Lynn began, her voice barely more than a whisper. I remember seeing how you and Dad loved each other—it was like magic. Is that love still here, even now?"

Belle's eyes met her daughter's, full of understanding and warmth. Her hands moved gracefully, forming words in the air with practiced ease. "The love your father and I shared was real, Lynn. It made you the woman you are today. We don't get to write our own stories, but we do get to live and appreciate them every day."

As Lynn watched her mother's hands dance with emotion, she felt a sense of clarity wash over her. She nodded, touched by her mother's wisdom. "Thank you, Mom," she signed back, a smile tugging at her lips.

Todd stood near the doorway, witnessing the mother and daughter exchange. He felt a pang of longing, remembering his childhood spent under Jazz and Mary's watchful care. His heart ached as he recalled the tender moments he shared with them before Mary passed.

"Dad," Todd said hesitantly, his voice thick with emotion. "How did you and Mom keep your love alive? How do you still feel it after all this time?"

Jazz turned his fading eyes toward his son, a smile spreading across his weathered face. "Son, love is like a river, always flowing and changing. Our love for your mother was wonderful, and as it moved along its path, we created great moments and a wonderful son. Love never stops moving, Todd. Even last night's storm was another part of the journey, adding to our life experiences."

Tears welled in Todd's eyes as he absorbed his father's words. He now understood that love had many forms and could be found even in the darkest times. "Thank you, Dad," he whispered, his voice cracking under gratitude.

As the room filled with warmth from the sunlight and the love between family, it seemed time stood still, allowing them to bask in the beauty of their connections and shared memories.

The room seemed to shimmer with an ethereal light in the tender glow of the afternoon sun. The air was thick with emotion, as if love had become tangible. Todd glanced over at Lynn, his brown eyes glistening with unshed tears. Her cheeks were flushed, and her long blonde hair framed her face like a halo. She looked so beautiful at that moment, her heart shining through every delicate feature.

"Hey," Todd murmured, his voice carrying the weight of his emotions.

"Hi," Lynn replied, her smile warm and inviting.

As Todd approached Lynn, he felt the pull of their connection, like an invisible thread drawing them closer. He hesitated for a heartbeat before closing the distance between them. With a gentle hand, he brushed a stray strand of hair from her face, tucking it carefully behind her ear.

"Can I...?" Todd's voice wavered, uncertainty flickering in his eyes.

Lynn nodded, her gaze locked on his. "Yes."

Todd leaned in, his lips brushing the softness of her cheek in a tender kiss. "If this is the only time I get to kiss you," he whispered, his breath warm against her skin, "I wanted it to be in this atmosphere full of love."

The intimacy of the moment washed over Lynn, leaving her breathless. She could feel the sincerity in his words, the depth of his emotions reaching out to her like a beacon. A warmth spread through her chest, filling her with a sense of belonging she hadn't realized she'd been missing.

"Thank you," Lynn whispered back, her voice barely audible. With a tender grace, she mirrored his actions, pressing her lips to his cheek in a chaste yet meaningful kiss.

As they pulled away, their gazes lingered, the vulnerability shared between them forging a bond that transcended the room. Todd's heart raced his thoughts a whirlwind of emotions and memories. He knew they were both caretakers for their parents, their lives intertwined with duty and love. But then, he allowed himself to imagine a future where they could share more than just stolen moments like these.

Lynn, too, felt a flutter of hope within her, a possibility she hadn't dared to consider before. Could there be more to life than what they had? In this atmosphere of love and understanding, she dared to dream of a world where their hearts could join, where the tender care they provided for their families could extend to each other.

"Whatever the future holds," Lynn said softly, her words a gentle promise, "I'm grateful for this moment."

"Me too," Todd agreed, his eyes shining with sincerity. "More than you know."

As they stood there, bathed in the golden light of love and family, it was as if time had paused, offering them a glimpse of an unwritten future. And although they couldn't predict what lay ahead, they knew they would face it together, hearts entwined by the love that now connected them.

Jazz released Belle from his embrace, and she smiled and signed, "I love you" to Lynn. Turning back to Jazz, her fingers danced gracefully, expressing her love for him.

"Love you too, Belle," Jazz's voice choked with emotion as he reciprocated her feelings.

All of the love and connections between everyone filled the room. Lynn couldn't help but smile, her eyes gleaming with joy at witnessing such a heartfelt moment. Though still reserved, Todd allowed a slight grin to grace his lips, touched by the love surrounding them.

"Come on, Todd," Lynn said softly, taking his hand. "Let's give them some privacy." With a gentle nod, they quietly slipped out of the room, leaving Jazz and Belle to embrace their significant moment fully.

The door shut, and silence settled over the living room again. Jazz and Belle sat there, their hands still intertwined, basking in the warmth and love that enveloped them.

A flood of emotions washed over Jazz as memories of their shared past flickered through his mind—dancing together under starlit skies, stolen kisses beneath old oak trees, and whispered promises of eternal love. Tears welled in his eyes as he comprehended the depth of Belle's love for him, threatening to spill onto his weathered cheeks.

"Jazz..." Belle murmured, her voice barely more than a whisper, yet it carried the weight of decades of love and longing. It was as if she understood the complexities of his heart, the way it ached with love and regret and still yearned for more.

"Darling, I've loved you all these years, and I'll continue loving you until my last breath," Jazz confessed, his voice cracking under the strain of his emotions. He leaned closer to Belle, their foreheads touching in a tender moment of shared vulnerability.

"Jazz, my love," Belle replied, her voice faint but filled with warmth, "I've always known how much you cared for me, even when I couldn't say the words myself. And now, here we are, with a second chance to cherish each other and make the most of our time together."

"Promise me, Belle," Jazz said through tear-filled eyes, "promise me that we'll never let go of this love we share."

"Jazz, I promise," she whispered, her breath brushing against his lips as they sealed their commitment with a soft, gentle kiss.

In that instant, as their hearts beat in unison, it was as if time had stopped. In the quiet sanctuary of Todd's living room, Jazz and Belle rediscovered the essence of true love—a love that had stood the test of time, defied the odds, and would continue to flourish for the rest of their lives.

Belle's eyes glistened like the first light of dawn as she looked at Jazz. Her hands, trembling slightly with emotion, continued to dance gracefully through the air, using sign language to convey her love and gratitude for everyone who had been by her side all these years. The delicate movements of her fingers painted a tapestry of warmth and sincerity that spoke louder than any words ever could.

"Jazz," Belle signed, her gaze locked onto his, "you have been my rock, my guiding light in the darkest times. Thank you for never giving up on me, even when I couldn't find the strength to speak."

Jazz's chest tightened, and he swallowed hard to keep his voice steady. He felt an overwhelming sense of humility and wonder at the love that radiated from Belle's every gesture. Trembling, his hands reached out to hers, enveloping them within his own.

As their intertwined hands formed a symbol of their unbreakable bond, the room seemed to glow with a warmth that went beyond mere physical sensation. This love transcended time and space, a deep and pure connection that felt like they were one being, two halves of a whole.

"Forever and always, Belle," Jazz whispered, his voice barely audible but filled with a conviction that could move mountains. "Forever and always."

From the doorway, Lynn watched the scene unfold, her eyes widening in astonishment as she saw her mother and Jazz holding each other so closely. She could feel the love radiating from their embrace, warming her from within as it washed over her like a tidal wave of pure happiness.

"Wow," she murmured under her breath, unable to tear her gaze away from the couple. It was rare to see such genuine affection, especially after so many years apart. Yet here were Jazz and Belle, proving that true love could indeed withstand the test of time.

"Mom, Jazz," Lynn called out gently, hesitant to interrupt their moment but eager to share in their joy. I can't say how happy I am to see you two like this. Your love is inspiring."

Belle and Jazz turned towards Lynn. Their faces flushed with emotion as they took in her words. Belle smiled warmly at her daughter, using sign language to express her gratitude for understanding and supporting their bond. Meanwhile, Jazz nodded, his eyes shimmering with unshed tears.

"Thank you, Lynn," Jazz said, his voice hoarse from the moment's emotions. "It means more to us than you could ever know."

"Your love and understanding mean the world to us," Belle signed, her eyes filled with warmth and sincerity.

Alone now, Jazz gently pulled away from Belle, holding her at arm's length as he gazed into her beautiful blue eyes. "Belle, I never thought we'd have this chance again... to be together like this."

"Neither did I, Jazz," Belle signed, her hands moving gracefully through the air as she spoke without words. "But we've been given this second chance and must cherish it."

"Absolutely," Jazz agreed, his heart swelling with love and determination. His mind raced with thoughts of all the moments they could share and the memories they could create together despite the obstacles life had thrown their way. "We'll make every moment count, my love."

"Promise me, Jazz," Belle signed, her eyes shining with emotion. "Promise me that we'll always fight for our love, no matter what comes our way."

"I promise, Belle," Jazz vowed, his voice choked with emotion. "I'll do whatever it takes to ensure we never lose each other again."

"Thank you, Jazz," Belle communicated, her hands trembling slightly with the weight of their commitment. "I love you."

"And I love you more than words can say," Jazz responded, his eyes brimming with tears as he contemplated their love and devotion.

The room seemed to hold its breath as Jazz and Belle sat silently, their hands still intertwined as if nothing could pry them apart. The sunlight filtering through the window cast a warm, golden glow on the two lovers, painting a picture of pure love transcending time and hardships.

"Can you believe it's us, Belle?" Jazz whispered his voice a mixture of wonder and awe. It was as if he was seeing everything anew, the colors brighter and the world more alive because of the woman sitting beside him.

Belle's fingers danced in reply, her smile radiant as she signed, "It feels like a dream, Jazz."

"More like a miracle," he corrected gently, his heart swelling with gratitude for this unexpected chance they'd been given.

As they sat there, wrapped in the warmth of their shared history and love, memories flitted like butterflies between them. They were no longer two solitary souls navigating the twilight of their lives but instead had found solace and strength in each other's presence.

Jazz's mind wandered briefly to the inevitable challenges they would face, his eyesight dimming with each passing day. But he pushed those thoughts away, focusing on the moment's beauty –how Belle's silver hair shimmered in the sunlight, and her blue eyes glistened with unspoken tenderness.

"Wow," he murmured, his heart aching with love for this incredible woman who had become his entire world. "Because I can't imagine my life without you."

As the sun dipped below the horizon, casting the room in a soft amber hue, Belle leaned her head on Jazz's shoulder. He could feel her heartbeat, steady and sure, the perfect counterpart to his own.

At that moment, the world seemed to crystallize around them – the warmth of their intertwined hands, the golden light washing over their faces, and the deep understanding that passed between them. As they basked in the love that filled the room, Jazz and Belle knew that their journey together had only just begun. And with each new sunrise, they would face it hand-in-hand, hearts beating as one, bound by a love that could triumph over any obstacle life sent their way.

Chapter 10

T odd and Lynn sat on the porch swing, their legs gently swaying in sync as they watched the fireflies dance in the warm summer air. The heavens painted the sky with hues of pink and orange as the sun dipped below the horizon, casting a soft glow over their intertwined fingers.

"When did you first notice how... close they've become?" Todd asked tentatively, keenly aware of Lynn's sensitivity when discussing her mother's emotions.

"I don't know," she replied. "But I thought it was because they're both such wonderful people, right? They deserve all the happiness in the world. And if being together brings them even a fraction of the joy we've found in each other, I couldn't be happier for them."

Todd smiled at Lynn's words, feeling his heart swell with love for her. He knew she was right —Belle and Jazz were kind-hearted souls who had experienced their fair share of hardships in life.

"Sometimes, I used to catch little hints from them that there was more to their story," he confided, his gaze never leaving the two silhouettes framed by the window. "I felt there was a secret the rest of us couldn't quite grasp."

"I did, too," Lynn agreed, her voice soft and full of wonder. "I'm just grateful that it led them here – to each other and us."

As the evening shadows deepened, Todd and Lynn were enveloped by the comforting silence that settled over them like a warm blanket. In those moments of quiet reflection, they found solace in the shared understanding that, though life was often unpredictable and filled with challenges, love guided them through even the darkest times.

This love that tethered their hearts and the bond between Belle and Jazz gave them hope for the future. In this future, happiness was attainable and something they could nurture and grow within the loving embrace of family.

The warm afternoon sun cast a golden glow upon the living room, illuminating the dust motes that danced lazily in the air. Lynn sat on the plush sofa, her nimble fingers tracing the intricate patterns of the embroidered throw pillow she held. The haunting melody of Jazz's saxophone drifted through the open window, harmonizing with the gentle rustling of leaves outside. It was a scene of contentment, yet Lynn could not shake the lingering curiosity ignited during her conversation with Todd.

"Mom," Lynn began hesitantly, gazing into Belle's blue eyes, which sparkled like sapphires in the sunlight. I've been thinking about what Todd said about you and Jazz. Is there...something more to your story?"

Belle's eyes seemed to hold a deep emotion, like an ocean of memories swirling beneath the surface. She raised her hands, signing with a fluid grace that belied her age: 'Fifty years is a long time.'

Lynn leaned forward, her heart quickening at the revelation. "What happened between you two?"

Belle's hands moved gracefully, telling a story that had long remained unspoken. 'We knew each other fifty years ago before life took us on separate paths.'

"Wow," Lynn breathed, her mind racing to process this unexpected information. "So, when did you realize that Jazz was from your past?"

With a tender smile, Belle signed her response. 'The moment they moved across the street. That's why I told you his son was checking you out. I knew if he were Jazz's son, he would have the potential to be a great man.'

"Mom, that's incredible," Lynn whispered, feeling a swell of emotion within her. "It's like fate brought you both together again."

As if on cue, Todd entered the room, his eyes alight with curiosity. "What's incredible?" he asked, settling down beside Lynn.

"Your dad and my mom," Lynn explained, her voice thick with emotion. "They knew fifty years couldn't stop anything."

"Really?" Todd asked, his eyebrows shooting up in surprise. "Why did you two never mention this before the storm?"

Belle's eyes shimmered with unshed tears as she signed her reply. 'Sometimes, it's easier to keep old memories locked away.'

Todd reached for his father's hand, his eyes glistening with empathy. "But now that we're all together, wouldn't it be nice to share those memories? To learn more about your history and how you felt about each other?"

Lynn nodded in agreement, placing a reassuring hand on Belle's shoulder. "We love you both so much, and knowing more about your past will bring us closer together as a family."

The room seemed to hold its breath as they awaited Belle's response. Finally, her hands moved slowly, carrying the weight of years' worth of silent memories. 'Yes,' she signed, her eyes filled with determination. 'It's time to share our story.'

The sound of a saxophone continued to weave its melancholic melody through the air. A profound connection settled over the room. They were a family bound by love, ready to embrace the past and journey together into the uncertain future.

The golden sunlight streamed down, casting a warm glow on the serene riverbank.

Jazz's salt and pepper hair danced in the wind as he looked around at the picturesque scene. He sighed, a contented sound, as he saw the flowing water and the lush greenery surrounding them. His eyes met Belle's, and she gave him an encouraging nod, her blue eyes shimmering with emotion.

"Your mother and I... we were young once, too, just like you two," Jazz began, his voice tinged with nostalgia. "We had our dreams, our hopes, and our fears."

Belle's hands fluttered gracefully, forming words without sound. 'And when I look at you both, I see so much of us, but better than we ever were.'

Lynn felt emotion wash over her as she listened to her mother's silent words. She could sense the bittersweet pride and sadness lingering behind those expressive eyes. Looking at Todd, she noticed a similar sentiment reflected in his gaze.

"Mom, Jazz," Lynn said hesitantly, her voice quivering with emotion. "What Todd and I have together is something we cherish deeply. But we're also afraid. We don't want to make the same mistakes, to let misunderstandings or miscommunications cost us years of happiness."

"Or even one year," Todd added, his jaw set with determination. "We want to learn from your experiences and to see if we can build a strong and loving life together."

Jazz's face softened as he regarded his son with pride. He reached out a hand to rest on Todd's shoulder, the gesture heavy with unspoken meaning. Belle's hands moved again, painting a picture of hope and understanding in the air.

'Our journey may have been filled with twists and turns, but if we can help you two avoid the same pitfalls, then our story will have a happy ending.

The river flowed on, its gentle current a symbol of the ever-changing nature of life. As they sat together beneath the dappled sunlight, four hearts beat in unison, bound by love and a shared desire to forge a brighter future.

Beneath the canopy of leaves, sunlight danced playfully on the water's surface, casting an ethereal glow upon the family gathered by the river. Jazz's warm smile seemed to mirror the light that shimmered around them, his eyes filled with the wisdom of years gone by.

"Communication," he said softly, his voice like a gentle breeze rustling through the trees. "That is the key, my dear children. The most important thing in any relationship is to be open and honest with one another."

Belle nodded emphatically, her blue eyes shining with unspoken words. Her hands began to move gracefully, the fluidity of her sign language echoing the serene flow of the river.

'Listen to each other,' she signed. 'When we were young, we made the mistake of assuming too much and speaking too little.'

"Sometimes it's the smallest misunderstandings that grow into insurmountable barriers," Jazz continued, his face clouding with memories of the past. "Fifty years ago, Belle and I disagreed with something so trivial... but our pride and a storm kept us from reconciling."

Todd and Lynn exchanged glances, their hearts heavy with the weight of their parents' lost years. They longed to understand, to learn from such heartache, and to create a love story that stood the test of time.

"Can you tell us more about what happened?" Todd ventured, his voice steady yet laced with curiosity. "We don't want to make the same mistakes."

Jazz sighed, his gaze drifting to the river as though it had answers to life's mysteries. "Our argument was about something as simple as where to spend our holidays. Can you believe that? But our stubbornness led us down separate paths, and it took us five decades to find our way back to one another."

"Yet, those years apart gave us families," Belle signed, her hands forming the words with equal parts grace and sorrow. And they taught us the importance of love."

"Indeed," Jazz agreed, his voice tinged with sadness and gratitude. "Though we lost precious time together, we gained a deeper understanding of love's true value. And now, we have all of you - our wonderful children."

Todd reached over and grasped Lynn's hand, their fingers intertwining like the roots of the trees that stood sentinel around them. In his eyes, she saw the promise of a love that would endure and grow stronger over time.

"Thank you," Lynn whispered, her voice barely audible above the gentle lapping of the river. "We will remember your lessons and hold onto them tightly as we think about a life together."

"Always communicate," Jazz reiterated, his gaze on his son and Lynn. "Speak from the heart, and let love guide you through every challenge that comes your way."

As the sun dipped lower in the sky, casting long shadows across the water, Todd and Lynn embraced the wisdom imparted by Jazz and Belle. They vowed never to let silence or pride separate them and to cherish each moment together, knowing that love was fragile and resilient – much like the river that flowed beside them.

Todd saw the myriad emotions playing across Lynn's face as they absorbed their parents' words. The past had been complicated, but there was hope for the future.

"Your story is incredibly moving," Lynn said, her voice soft and empathic. "I can only imagine how difficult it must have been for both of you. But look at us now, sitting together as a family."

"Exactly," Todd agreed, his eyes locking onto Jazz's. "Our love for each other wouldn't exist without the paths you two walked. In a way, your lost time brought us to this moment."

Tears shimmered in Jazz's eyes, but he smiled warmly, the corners of his mouth lifting with understanding. "Happiness is often found in the most unexpected places, sometimes after many years. Don't worry about us, my children. Love still won, and we're good."

Todd felt gratitude wash over him, and he squeezed Lynn's hand tighter. They shared a knowing glance, realizing that every twist and turn had led them to each other.

"Thank you for sharing your story with us," Todd said, his voice thick with emotion. "We'll learn from it and always keep communication open."

Lynn nodded, wiping away a tear that had escaped her eye. "We promise to honor your journey by making ours the best it can be. Our love will grow stronger, day by day."

Jazz's gaze held a depth of wisdom earned through decades of life experience. "That's all we could ever ask for," he said softly, his voice carrying on the gentle breeze that rustled the leaves overhead.

Todd and Lynn sat beside their parents, hearts entwined in a promise never to let love slip through their fingers like sand. The past may have been filled with lost opportunities, but the future held endless possibilities - and that was something they all could cherish.

The world around them seemed still, offering a tender moment of serenity amidst the soft rustle of leaves and birdsong.

"Thank you," Lynn whispered, her eyes shining with unshed tears as she looked at Todd. "For everything. For being here and helping me see that we can grow from our parents' past."

Todd's thumb traced gentle circles on the back of her hand, his heart swelling with love for the woman beside him. "Our love is our own, Lynn," he said softly, barely above a murmur. "We can create something beautiful together that lasts a lifetime and beyond."

A sudden hush fell over the woods as if nature held its breath in anticipation. Then, as a secret was unveiled, musicians and singers emerged from the trees, their melodies weaving together to form a symphony of love and hope. Lynn's eyes widened in surprise, and her hand instinctively moved to cover her mouth.

"Wha-what's happening?" she stammered, clearly taken aback by the unexpected turn of events.

Todd smiled at her, his love and devotion evident in every line of his face. "I've been thinking about this for a while," he admitted, his voice filled with emotion. "You mean more to me than words can express, Lynn. And I don't want to wait another fifty years, or even another fifty seconds, to make you mine."

As the music swelled around them, Todd slowly lowered himself onto one knee, never breaking eye contact with Lynn. Her breath caught in her throat, her eyes welling with tears as she realized the moment's gravity.

"Will you marry me, Lynn?" Todd asked, his voice steady despite the whirlwind of emotions threatening to overwhelm him. "Will you be my wife, for now, and always, so we never lose another precious moment together?"

Lynn stared at him, her heart pounding in her chest as she took in the love and sincerity in his eyes. Unable to speak, she nodded, tears streaming down her cheeks in a torrent of joy and gratitude. Todd rose and gently embraced her, their hearts beating in unison as they shared a tender, loving kiss.

Jazz and Belle watched with shimmering eyes, deeply moved by the powerful display of love before them. They saw themselves reflected in Todd and Lynn, echoes of a love that had once been lost but now found again in their children's hearts. And as the music continued to play, the river carried their hopes and dreams along its timeless current, weaving a tapestry of love that would endure for generations.

The music from the woods had quieted, replaced by the gentle rustling of leaves and the soothing lullaby of the flowing water. Todd and Lynn, still locked in their tender embrace, seemed to exist in a world of their own, each heartbeat a testament to the love that bound them together.

"Such a beautiful moment," Jazz whispered, his voice thick with emotion. He blinked away the tears that blurred his already failing vision, a bittersweet mixture of joy and nostalgia washing over him. "I couldn't be prouder, son."

Todd pulled back from Lynn, turning to face his father with a grateful smile. "Thanks, Dad. It means a lot to hear you say that."

"Your mother would have loved this," Jazz continued, now focused on Lynn. "And I know Belle feels the same way." He paused, a pensive expression crossing his features as he contemplated his following words. "You're a better man than I am, Todd. I never got to do this like you did."

"Dad, don't—" Todd began, but his father held up a hand to silence him.

"Let me finish. I want you both to know how much I admire your courage and your love for one another. And I hope... I hope you'll learn from our mistakes and keep the lines of communication open between you."

"Thank you, Jazz," Lynn said softly, squeezing his hand. "We promise to do our best."

A sudden surge of energy seemed to course through Belle at Jazz's heartfelt words. She approached Todd and Lynn, her blue eyes shimmering with unshed tears. With great effort, she leaned forward and pressed a tender kiss to each of their cheeks, then gathered her strength to whisper, "I love you both, and I wish you a forever of tomorrows."

Todd and Lynn exchanged glances, their hearts overflowing with gratitude for Jazz and Belle's blessings. They knew they were fortunate to have found each other and vowed, in that moment, to cherish every day they were given together.

"Thank you, Belle," Todd murmured, his voice choked with emotion. "We'll make the most of every precious moment."

"Your love and support mean everything to us," Lynn added, her eyes shining with tears. "We promise to honor your legacy and build a future filled with love and happiness."

The past may have been filled with heartache and loss, but the future promised new beginnings – and a love that would transcend time itself.

The setting sun's golden rays glow warmly on the riverside, illuminating Belle's silver hair as she stands before Todd and Lynn. The emotion in her eyes reflected the depth of the love that had gathered them all there.

"Mom," Lynn said softly, touching her mother's arm in gratitude. Her heart swelled with love for this firm, silent woman who had brought so much love into their lives.

Belle withdrew her hand from Lynn's grasp but only to begin using sign language, her fingers moving gracefully through the air. "We have a wedding to plan," she signed, her eyes twinkling with excitement.

Todd laughed, tears still clinging to his lashes. "You're right, Belle. We can't forget about that."

"Weddings are all about bringing people together, after all," Lynn added, her voice shimmering with happiness.

As they stood there, surrounded by their family, Todd couldn't help but marvel at how life unfolded. It was as if everything had led them to this pivotal time when their love would be celebrated and their future as one would begin.

"Thank you, Belle," he whispered, his voice thick with gratitude. "We'll ensure it's a day we all remember forever."

"Speaking of which," Jazz interjected, a mischievous glint in his eye, "I might know a few musicians who'd love to play for our big day."

"Really?" Lynn asked, her eyes widening with delight. "That would be perfect!"

"Nothing is too good for my son and future daughter-in-law," Jazz replied, his chest swelling with pride.

Todd glanced around at the faces of those he loved – his father, Jazz, Belle, and his soon-to-be wife, Lynn. He felt a surge of determination well up within him, a promise to himself and his loved ones that he would never let the past repeat itself.

"Let's make this wedding a symbol of our love," he thought, "and a testament to the power of communication and understanding. We'll carry these lessons with us for the rest of our lives."

Todd and Lynn stood hand in hand – ready to plan their future together, strengthened by the love and wisdom of those who had come before them.

Chapter 11

J azz Montgomery sat alone in his room, the dim glow of the bedside lamp casting shadows on the walls. His once-keen eyes struggled to bring the world into focus, and he clenched his hands into fists, feeling the familiar frustration rise within him. At the same time, Jazz stared at the blurred photograph of Belle Thompson on the nightstand, her beautiful blue eyes just a hazy memory. He longed to see her face again, to look into her eyes without the veil of his failing vision.

"Please," he whispered to no one in particular, "don't let this come between me and Belle."

The door creaked open gently, revealing the stocky silhouette of Thomas "Tom" Davis, Jazz's oldest friend and best man at his wedding to his late wife, Mary. Tom stepped inside, concern etched on his face as he observed his friend's distress.

"Jazz," Tom said softly, "I heard you talking to yourself. What's going on, old friend?"

Jazz sighed and rubbed his weary eyes. "It's my eyesight, Tom. It's worsening daily, and I'm scared it'll burden Belle."

Tom crossed the room and settled into the armchair beside Jazz's bed. He leaned forward, resting his elbows on his knees. "You know, Jazz, I've seen you overcome so many challenges in your life. But this... this is just another hurdle to cross, not a burden for anyone."

"Easy for you to say," Jazz muttered, looking away. He knew Tom meant well, but his words did little to ease his anxiety.

"Look at me, Jazz," Tom insisted, waiting until his friend reluctantly met his gaze. "I know that losing your sight must be difficult. But that doesn't change who you are or what you mean to people, especially Belle. She loves you, Jazz. And that love runs deeper than any physical ability."

Jazz clenched his jaw as he fought against the emotions rising within him. He knew Tom was right, but that didn't make his fear less accurate. "I just... I want to be there for her, Tom. I want her to smile and know I'm not holding her back."

"Trust me," Tom said with a warm, knowing smile. "You could never hold Belle back. She's always seen your strength, even when you couldn't. Your eyesight might fade, but your heart and soul are still strong."

Jazz nodded slowly, allowing Tom's words to sink in. It wouldn't be easy, but love was more profound than his body's limitations. And if anyone could help him navigate this new chapter in life, it was Belle.

Jazz's hands trembled as he traced the lines on his palm, feeling the weight of every passing year. Tom sat beside him, a quiet and steady presence that offered comfort amid uncertainty.

"Tom," Jazz began, his voice barely above a whisper. "I'm scared."

"Of losing your eyesight?" Tom asked gently, placing a hand on Jazz's shoulder.

"Of losing everything," Jazz admitted, his eyes filling with unshed tears. "I never thought I'd feel this way again, not after so many years... But seeing Belle, it's like discovering a part of me I didn't know was still alive."

"Life has a funny way of doing that, huh?" Tom mused, his own eyes reflecting the memories of the past. "You've always had a special connection with Belle, even back then. She brought out something in you that no one else could."

"Love," Jazz said softly, his heart aching with the memory of their first meeting. "She taught me how to love, and I carried that with me when I met Mary. All these years later, I still can't believe how lucky I was to have them both in my life."

"Maybe there's a reason for that," Tom suggested, his gaze steady and wise. "Maybe life wanted you to learn more about love, so it brought you back to Belle, where it all started."

Jazz considered Tom's words, his mind racing with possibilities. He knew that love was a powerful force, capable of weathering any storm – but could it truly overcome the darkness that threatened to swallow him whole?

"Tom," Jazz said, determination shining through his fear. "I want to believe that. I want to believe that love can conquer anything – even this. But what if it isn't enough? What if I'm not enough?"

"Jazz, listen to me," Tom said earnestly, his voice solid and reassuring. "You have always been enough – for Belle, Mary, and everyone who has ever known you. Your eyesight might be fading, but that doesn't change the man you are."

"Your heart is what drew Belle to you all those years ago, and it's what keeps her by your side now," Tom continued, a gentle smile playing at the corners of his lips. "Love isn't about what you can see or touch; it's about the connection between two souls. And in that regard, Jazz, you have more than enough to give."

Jazz felt the warmth of Tom's words seep into his very being, soothing the fear that threatened to consume him. He knew Tom was right – love wasn't just about the physical. It was about the emotional bond that united them.

"Thank you, Tom," Jazz said, his voice filled with gratitude. I don't know what I would do without your wisdom and friendship."

"Let's not find out, okay?" Tom replied with a chuckle, reassuringly squeezing Jazz's shoulder.

As Jazz sat with Tom, his mind wandered to Belle and the life they could share. His eyes might be failing him, but his heart was strong, and together, they would face whatever challenges lay ahead. For love, he realized, was indeed the greatest gift of all.

Belle sat at her tiny writing desk, the lamp's soft glow casting a gentle light over the delicate stationery before her. The pen felt like an extension of her heart as she poured her emotions onto the paper, her beautiful blue eyes brimming with unspoken words and feelings.

"Dearest Jazz," she began, shaking her hand as she wrote. I cannot express how thankful I am for this unexpected chapter in our lives. To be reunited after all these years feels like a miracle, and I cherish every moment we spend together."

Her memories danced across the page, recounting shared laughter and whispered conversations, the warmth of his hand on hers, and how he had always made her feel seen and understood. Belle paused, her pen hovering above the paper as she debated whether to reveal the depths of her feelings. She bit her lip, her heart heavy with uncertainty.

"Mom?" Lynn's voice interrupted her thoughts, and Belle looked up to see her daughter standing in the doorway, concern etched on her face.

"Are you okay?" Lynn asked, walking over to sit beside Belle, her warm smile comforting.

"Jazz means so much to me, but I'm afraid," Belle signed, her hands trembling with emotion. "What if our best days are behind us? What if he thinks I'm foolish for feeling this way?"

"Mom, you know that's not true," Lynn replied. "He adores you; I can see how he looks at you."

Belle hesitated, then handed the letter to Lynn. Her daughter read it, tears filling her eyes as the depth of her mother's love shone through in every word.

"Jazz needs to have this letter from you, Mom," Lynn said firmly, taking her mother's hand. "Trust me, he'll treasure it."

Together, they walked across the street, the crisp evening air whispering around them like a promise of hope. As they approached Jazz and Todd's porch, Belle's heart raced with anticipation and fear.

"Everything will be okay, Mom," Lynn whispered. "Love is worth taking risks for."

Belle nodded, watching as her daughter carefully placed the letter on the porch, and they returned home. As they stood on their porch, Belle clung to the hope that Jazz would understand her heart and cherish the love she was offering.

"Your eyesight doesn't determine your worth, my friend," Tom reassured him, leaning forward in his chair. "You have so much to offer, not just to Belle but to everyone around you."

Jazz's fingers traced the frayed edge of the blanket, his thoughts swirling like autumn leaves caught in a gust of wind. What did he have to offer? He was no longer the young man he had been when he first met Belle, full of dreams and ambitions. Time had weathered him, carved lines into his face that told stories he would rather forget.

"Jazz, listen to me," Tom said, his voice stern yet compassionate. "You are a good man - one of the best I've ever known. Belle sees that and loves you for who you are, not what you can or can't do."

"Tom, how can you say that with such certainty? That's fifty years, and now I'm this broken shell of a man." Jazz's words came out harsher than He intended, and frustration simmered beneath the surface.

"Because I saw it in her eyes years ago, Jazz." Tom leaned back in his chair, his gaze steady and unwavering. When she looked at you, the world stopped momentarily; all that matters is your connection."

"Maybe you're right," Jazz conceded, his heart aching with longing. "But how do I know that this isn't just nostalgia speaking? What if we're both chasing after ghosts of who we used to be?"

"Jazz, sometimes love comes back to us when we least expect it," Tom said softly, his eyes filled with wisdom. "You don't have to have all the answers right now. Just take one step at a time, and let life unfold as it will."

The room seemed to hold its breath as Jazz considered Tom's words, the hazy orange light giving way to the deep blues of twilight. A new resolve flickered in Jazz's chest like the first spark of a fire.

"Whatever happens, I know my love story started with her," Jazz murmured, his voice tinged with determination. "And from the look of things, it's going to end with her too."

"Then go to her, Jazz," Tom encouraged him, a warm smile on his lips. "Trust in the love you share, and let it guide you through this new chapter of your lives."

"Thank you, Tom," Jazz whispered, his newfound hope brighter than any star in the evening sky. "I won't let fear hold me back any longer."

Belle's heart pounded as she took a deep breath, gathering the courage as she waited on her porch. Gripping the edges of her cardigan tightly around her, Belle settled into the wicker chair and anxiously watched Jazz's house across the street.

Her eyes darted between the letter Lynn had left on Jazz's porch and the front door, worrying her bottom lip as she thought about what she had written. Would he understand her feelings? Would he still want to be a part of her life even though they were both in the twilight of their years? She could only hope.

"Mom," Lynn's gentle voice called from inside the house, "you okay?"

Belle nodded, giving her daughter a small smile before gazing at Jazz's home. She knew she wouldn't be able to hear his reaction, but she wanted to be there when he discovered her letter, to share in this vulnerable moment between them.

Jazz stepped onto his porch, his cane tapping softly on the wooden floorboards. He paused, sensing something out of the ordinary. A slight breeze rustled the leaves around him, carrying a faint scent of lavender – Belle's signature perfume. The sweet fragrance tugged at his heartstrings, reminding him of countless moments they'd spent together so many years ago.

He moved forward cautiously, feeling for the edge of the porch swing before sitting down. His fingers brushed against the crisp paper of Belle's letter, and he felt a rush of surprise and happiness. Even though his vision was limited, he could sense the love and sincerity that had gone into every word.

"Is this...?" Jazz whispered to himself, his voice choked with emotion. He traced the elegant loops of Belle's handwriting, his heart swelling with gratitude. How lucky he was to have someone like her in his life again.

Belle watched as Jazz opened her letter, her nerves tangling with excitement. Though he couldn't see her face clearly across the street, he could feel the warmth radiating from her, like two souls connected by an invisible thread. Belle felt tears prick at the corners of her eyes, overwhelmed by the beauty of their love story continuing to unfold.

Jazz and Belle sat on their respective porches as the night deepened, linked by shared memories and renewed hope. At that moment, they knew their love would guide them no matter the challenges. And with that knowledge burning brightly in their hearts, they faced the future hand in hand, ready for whatever it may bring.

Jazz's hands trembled as he unfolded the letter, the delicate paper rustling softly in the evening breeze. He squinted at the words, his failing eyesight making it difficult to read, but as soon as he deciphered the first line, he was transported back in time.

"Dear Jazz," Belle wrote, "our love story began more than half a century ago, and though we took different paths, our hearts remained connected."

"Connected," Jazz repeated under his breath, feeling the weight of that single word. He could sense the love and sincerity that had gone into every dish.

"Every day I spent away from you felt like an eternity, but now that we've found each other again, I know we can face anything together," Belle's letter continued. "Our love is a beacon that will guide us through the darkest times, and I am grateful for every moment we share."

"Beacon" – love as a guiding light, Jazz thought. His chest tightened, an unfamiliar vulnerability settling within him. Was it possible to feel so much emotion all at once? He blinked away tears, his vision blurring further.

"Thank you, Belle," Jazz murmured, the words barely audible. He held the letter close to his heart, cherishing each heartfelt word and the woman who had written it.

"Time may have changed us, but our love remains steadfast. We are stronger together, Jazz and our journey has just begun. Yours always, Belle."

"Always," Jazz whispered, the word resonating deep within him. He stood up slowly, a newfound determination filling his being. He looked across the street towards Lynn and Belle's home, his heart full of love and gratitude.

"Always," he said once more, louder this time. He kissed the letter gently before tucking it into his pocket, a warm sensation spreading through his chest.

With one last lingering look at Belle's house, Jazz turned towards his front door, ready to face whatever the future held for them. Their love story had started with her, and now he knew it would end with her too – and that was all that mattered.

Chapter 12

The warm afternoon sun cast a golden hue over Jazz's porch as he squinted, trying to make out the familiar path to Belle's house. His eyesight had worsened lately, making every step like a leap of faith.

"Jazz?" Belle mouthed softly from across the way, her hands shaping the words in the air as she noticed his struggle. Her blue eyes sparkled with concern as she hurried toward him, silver hair flowing behind her.

"Hey, beautiful," Jazz greeted her with a warm smile, feeling a sense of relief wash over him as she reached out and took his arm. "I was just coming to see you."

"Let's go back to my place," Belle said through her elegant hand gestures, her eyes radiating love and understanding.

Together, they slowly made their way to Belle's garden, the vibrant colors of the flowers blending into an impressionistic painting as Jazz's vision blurred. They settled on a wooden bench, nestled between blooming roses and wisteria vines that gently swayed in the breeze.

"Your garden is still so lovely, Belle," Jazz murmured, feeling the soft petals brush against his skin. "I can only imagine the true beauty of how it looks even though I can still see some of it."

Belle squeezed his hand reassuringly, her silence conveying the warmth and compassion that he cherished. Jazz lulled into a peaceful slumber, with Belle's head nestled against his shoulder.

"Jazz, wake up," Belle gently signed when he started to stir. The orange hues of sunset painted the sky, and Jazz blinked groggily, realizing that his vision had worsened even further.

"Is it evening already?" he asked, rubbing his eyes as if it would somehow clear his sight. Belle nodded, her eyes etched with worry.

"Thank you for waking me. I should probably head home now," Jazz said, attempting to stand and navigate his surroundings. But the world seemed a confusing mass of colors and shapes, leaving him disoriented and uncertain.

"Here, let me help you," Belle offered, looping her arm through his and steadying him as he took a shaky step forward. Her touch was a lifeline in this increasingly unfamiliar world, and Jazz clung to it, grateful for her unwavering support.

As they began their slow walk back, Jazz couldn't help but feel a growing dread, wondering how he would manage in a world that was slipping away from him. He glanced at Belle, her eyes filled with determination and love, and knew that no matter what challenges lay ahead, they would face them together.

Jazz hesitated, his fingers hovering over the smooth petals of a rose that seemed to blur and merge with the green leaves behind it. He felt Belle's arm tighten around his, her presence a reassuring anchor as he struggled to make sense of the dimming world.

"Let's go inside," Belle signed, her fingers dancing in front of him like fireflies in the dusk. "Todd and Lynn are at work, so we have plenty of time together. And they expect us to be here now anyway." She paused, giving Jazz a tender smile. "Besides, I love every moment with you."

"Thank you," Jazz whispered, allowing himself to be guided inside her cozy home. In his present state, the once-familiar surroundings now appeared foreign, yet somehow comforting, with the faint scent of lavender wafting from a nearby vase.

In the warm embrace of Belle's kitchen, Jazz sat at the table while she busied herself making lunch. The rhythmic sounds of her chopping vegetables and the steam rising from the pot on the stove created a symphony of sensation that grounded him even as his vision betrayed him.

"I'm scared, Belle," Jazz confessed, staring at the blurry outline of her face while she stirred a pot on the stove. "I don't know how much worse this will get or how I'll manage when...when I can't see anything at all."

Belle set down her wooden spoon and moved closer, resting a hand on his shoulder. Her eyes locked onto his, shining with empathy and understanding. Her fingers formed gentle words in the air: "It's okay to be afraid. But remember, you're not alone. I'm here for you."

"Your support means everything to me," Jazz said, his voice cracking with emotion. "But I can't help feeling like I'm becoming a burden to you and my son."

"Never," Belle signed fiercely, shaking her head. "You are a gift, Jazz. And we'll navigate this together."

As they ate their meal, Jazz found solace in the rich flavors of Belle's cooking, each bite a testament to her unwavering care and love. He marveled at how she could communicate so much with her hands and eyes and wondered if he could find new ways to connect with the world around him.

"Maybe I could learn to read braille," he mused aloud, a tiny spark of determination flickering in his chest. "Or find other ways to experience things without relying on my sight."

Belle smiled, her eyes warm and encouraging. She signed, "We can do it together. Whatever comes our way, we'll face it hand in hand."

Jazz felt renewed hope as the last rays of sunlight filtered through the kitchen window. Though the future remained uncertain, he knew they would weather the storm as one with Belle by his side. He found the strength to face the darkness ahead within the sanctuary of her embrace.

Jazz felt the weight of Belle's care and concern with every gentle clink of dishes. As she cleaned up the remnants of their meal, he couldn't help but watch her graceful movements, her silver hair catching the light, casting a halo around her. He could feel her love for him as tangible as a warm embrace.

"Jazz," Belle signed, pausing in her work, her eyes softening with determination. "I think we should visit an eye specialist. There might be something they can do to help."

He hesitated, his heart torn between hope and dread. Could there be a solution for his failing eyesight? "Do you think they'll be able to help me?" he asked, his voice barely above a whisper.

Belle nodded, her blue eyes filled with optimism. "We won't know until we try," she signed, her hands moving fluidly through the air. "And I want to make sure we explore every possible option."

Her words, her unwavering belief in him, steeled his resolve. "All right," he agreed, nodding firmly. "Let's schedule an appointment."

A smile of relief graced her lips, and she crossed the kitchen to retrieve a calendar hanging on the wall. Jazz marveled at how effortlessly Belle took charge of the situation, her slender fingers on the keys of the computer and jotting down details. He felt grateful she was here, guiding him through this unfamiliar territory.

"Done," Belle signed after moving away from the computer, the corners of her mouth turning in a small, triumphant smile. "I've scheduled an appointment for us, and I'll arrange transportation to the doctor's office."

"Thank you, Belle," Jazz murmured, his chest swelling with love and admiration for the woman who had become his rock. Inwardly, he wondered if he could ever repay her for all the support and care she had given him.

As Belle returned to the sink, a wave of determination washed over Jazz. He would not let this challenge defeat him. With Belle by his side, they would face whatever the future held together. And as he watched her hands, so gentle yet firm, he knew that together, they would find a way through the darkness.

Jazz stared at the eye chart, or more accurately, where he knew it hung on the wall, his vision too blurry to discern the letters. The sterile scent of the eye specialist's office mingled with a faint hint of disinfectant and leather from the examination chair. He gripped the armrests, feeling the cold metal beneath his fingers, as Belle stood beside him, her soft but steady presence providing comfort.

"All right, Mr. Montgomery," Dr. Patel said, her voice warm yet professional. "I will perform a few tests to determine the extent of your vision loss."

"Of course," Jazz replied, swallowing hard and trying to focus on the sound of her footsteps as she crossed the room.

"Can you make out any letters on the chart?" Dr. Patel asked, gesturing toward the indistinct blur on the wall.

"Unfortunately, no," Jazz admitted, his heart aching with frustration.

"All right, let's move on to some other tests." Dr. Patel spent the next several minutes conducting various examinations, from shining lights into his eyes to testing his peripheral vision.

As the tests progressed, Jazz couldn't help but feel a mounting dread. Each failed attempt weighed heavily on him. He glanced at Belle, taking solace in her reassuring smile even as he struggled to see it.

"Mr. Montgomery," Dr. Patel began, her tone gentle as she came to stand before them. "I've completed my assessment, and I'm afraid your condition is irreversible."

Jazz felt his breath catch in his throat, the words hitting him like a punch to the gut. "So, there's nothing that can be done?"

"Your eyesight will continue to deteriorate, and eventually, you will lose it completely," she confirmed, her gaze sympathetic. "But I must emphasize that this doesn't have to define your life. Many people live fulfilling lives despite vision loss."

"Thank you, Dr. Patel," Jazz murmured, struggling to keep his voice steady as he turned to Belle, her blurry figure a beacon of hope. "We'll find a way to adapt."

"Of course," she signed, her hands conveying a steadfast determination that filled him with gratitude and love.

As they left the doctor's office hand in hand, Jazz's thoughts churned like a stormy sea. How would he navigate this new world? How could he bear to live daily without seeing Belle's face or the beauty of her garden?

But as they stepped outside, the sun's warmth on his skin and Belle's fingers intertwined with his own, he realized that whatever darkness lay ahead, their love would be the light that guided them both. And together, they would face this uncertain future unafraid.

The sun cast an amber glow on Belle's silver hair as they sat together on the park bench, a gentle breeze rustling the leaves above them. Jazz closed his eyes, knowing that each passing moment brought him closer to darkness. But for now, he focused on the warmth of Belle's body pressed against his, her fingers tracing patterns on the back of his hand.

"Jazz," she signed, her blue eyes brimming with unshed tears, "you know I'll always be here for you, right?"

"Of course, Belle," he replied softly, his voice quivering with emotion. "But I can't help worrying about the future."

"Let's not think about that now." She signed, her hands forming words that shone through his dimming vision like beacons of hope. "We'll face it one day at a time, together."

Jazz swallowed the lump in his throat, trying to find strength in her unwavering love. He looked around, taking in the vibrant colors of the park – the fire-red leaves of the maple trees, the golden hues of the sun reflecting off the pond – wondering how long it would be before these sights were only a distant memory.

"Thank you, Belle," he whispered, turning to look deep into her eyes, hoping she could read the depth of his gratitude behind the growing veil. "You are my rock, my solace. I don't know what I'd do without you."

Belle's eyes shimmered with emotion as she leaned in and pressed her forehead against his. He felt the warmth of her breath on his skin, the gentle pressure of her lips as they shared a tender, loving kiss.

"Promise me something, Jazz," she signed when they finally pulled apart, her hands moving with a desperate urgency. "Promise me that no matter what happens, we will always find a way to communicate and share our love."

"Of course, Belle," Jazz vowed, his heart swelling with love and determination. "We will always find a way."

As they sat together on that park bench, the world slowly fading around them, Jazz and Belle found solace in their shared love and connection. Jazz knew that Belle would guide him no matter what darkness lay ahead.

Jazz and Belle sat in the garden. The vibrant colors of the flowers seemed to dance in the gentle breeze, their sweet fragrance filling the air. Jazz closed his eyes momentarily, savoring the feeling of Belle's hand in his – her fingers intertwined with his, providing a lifeline amidst the uncertainty.

"Jazz," Belle signed, her hands moving gracefully with every word, "I want you to know I'll always be by your side. Our love is strong enough."

Jazz's heart swelled with gratitude for Belle's unwavering support. He looked into her deep blue eyes, seeing the sincerity behind her words. "Thank you, Belle," he said softly, gently squeezing her hand. "Your love means more to me than anything else."

Jazz couldn't help but marvel at the strength of their connection. Despite their challenges, Belle was a constant source of comfort and reassurance.

"Would you like some tea?" Belle signed, her fingers brushing against Jazz gently. He nodded, grateful for the simple gesture of care.

As Belle rose to prepare the tea, Jazz watched her move about the kitchen with ease. How she navigated the space without relying on words reminded him of their unique bond. It was as if they communicated through an unspoken language transcending the limitations of sight and sound.

Returning with two steaming cups of tea, Belle settled back beside Jazz, their hands instinctively finding each other again. They sipped their tea in

Jazz and Belle sat side by side on the porch swing in the golden light of the setting sun. The warm breeze carried the scent of freshly bloomed flowers from Belle's garden, surrounding them with serenity. Jazz took a deep breath, feeling his chest expand with something more than just air – it was hope.

"Believe it or not," Jazz began, his voice gentle as a whisper, "I've always been afraid of the dark. But that fear seems to fade away with you by my side."

Belle turned her gaze towards him, her expressive blue eyes shimmering with warmth and understanding. She brushed a stray strand of Jazz's salt and pepper hair behind his ear, her fingers lingering momentarily on his cheek.

"Because, Belle, you're my guiding light in the darkness," he continued, no longer looking at her but staring into the distance as if seeing their future together. "And I know that even when my world turns completely black, we'll still find a way to communicate."

His hands trembled slightly as he took hold of the beginner's braille book they had bought earlier that day. He opened it and hesitantly traced his fingers over the embossed dots, trying to decipher the hidden messages within.

"Even if I can't see your beautiful face anymore, I'll still feel your love through your touch, and our connection will never be lost," Jazz said, his determination evident in the furrow of his brow.

Belle's eyes glistened with unshed tears as she placed her hand over Jazz's, guiding his fingers along the lines of raised dots. Her gentle yet firm touch supported him in learning this new language. As they worked together, Jazz began recognizing the patterns beneath his fingertips, each dot transforming from a foreign symbol into a meaningful letter.

"See, Jazz?" Belle signed, her hands and fingers dancing like graceful butterflies. "You're already making progress. We'll face this together, and our love will guide us."

Jazz felt gratitude and love flow through him as he watched Belle's hands form each word. Her unwavering commitment to their journey was his anchor, keeping him grounded in the present while giving him the courage to face the unknown.

"Thank you," he whispered, turning to Belle with teary eyes. He leaned forward and pressed his lips to her forehead, a tender kiss that spoke volumes of his love for her.

Jazz and Belle continued their braille lesson as the sun dipped below the horizon, their fingers intertwining and moving in unison over the pages. Together, they forged a path through the darkness, guided by the unwavering light of their love.

The sun cast a warm, golden glow over Belle's garden as Jazz traced the last line of raised dots on the braille page. He glanced up at Belle, her silver hair shimmering like a halo in the sunlight, and marveled at the strength they drew from one another. The vibrant colors of the flowers surrounding them seemed to intensify as if nature was celebrating the love that bound their hearts together.

"Did I get it right?" Jazz asked, his voice tinged with excitement and uncertainty.

Belle nodded, her blue eyes sparkling with pride. She signed, "Yes, you did. I knew you had it in you."

Jazz's heart swelled with gratitude as he watched the fluid movements of her hands, each gesture imbuing him with newfound confidence. He looked down at the braille book before him, realizing that even though his world was shrinking, Belle was helping him expand it in ways he never thought possible.

"Thank you," Jazz whispered, his eyes glistening with emotion. "You've given me hope, Belle. Even when my sight fades completely, our love will remain a constant light in the darkness."

Belle reached for Jazz's hand, intertwining their fingers as she signed, "And I'll be right by your side every step."

As they sat hand in hand, Jazz couldn't help but reflect on the journey that had brought them to this point.

The fear and frustration he felt when his vision began to deteriorate had threatened to envelop him, but Belle's unwavering presence had kept him afloat. He had found solace and understanding in her; her love had become both an anchor and a beacon to guide him through the coming storm.

"Let's go for a walk," he suggested, feeling the need to savor the beauty of their surroundings while he still could. "I want to memorize every inch of this garden to carry it with me."

Belle smiled, her eyes reflecting the love and determination that fueled their shared journey. Hand in hand, they rose from the bench and began to navigate the garden's winding paths, pausing to admire the delicate blooms and breathe in their sweet fragrance.

With each step, Jazz committed the feel of the earth beneath his feet and the sound of Belle's laughter to memory, knowing that these moments would become precious treasures in the coming days. As they walked, the sun dipped lower in the sky, casting long shadows across the garden and bathing everything in a soft, golden light.

For Jazz and Belle, the fading light represented not an end but a new beginning. Together, they would face the coming darkness hand in hand, their love providing the strength and courage they needed to embrace the uncertain future with open hearts.

Chapter 13

The comfortable couches and armchairs beckoned the family to gather together. Todd and Lynn exchanged glances before ushering their respective parents, Jazz and Belle, to sit down. The room was filled with soft, inviting colors, and photographs of their lives together adorned the walls, creating a safe and comfortable space for discussion.

"Mom, Dad," Todd began, rubbing his hands together nervously, "Lynn and I noticed that something seemed a bit off today. You both don't seem to have that usual glow of love we're used to seeing." He hesitated momentarily, searching their faces for any sign of what might be troubling them.

Jazz shifted in his seat, his salt and pepper hair catching the fading sunlight streaming through the window. His warm smile faltered, just enough for Todd to notice. Belle's expressive blue eyes flitted between Jazz and daughter, her silver hair framing her face like a halo. She gave a slight nod, acknowledging her future son-in-law's observation.

"Is everything all right?" Todd continued, concern etched into his strong jawline. Lynn reached out, gently placing her hand on her mother's arm, her blonde curls shimmering under the soft lamplight. She mirrored Todd's concerned expression but remained silent, allowing him to lead the conversation.

Jazz heaved, his tall, lean frame sinking further into the plush cushions of the chair. "I suppose there's no hiding it from you two, huh?" he said softly, a small chuckle escaping his lips.

"Come on, Dad. We're all here for each other," Todd encouraged, forcing a reassuring smile. Looking around at the faces of those he held dear, he couldn't help but think about the legacy of love they were building together.

"All right," Jazz conceded, his warm smile returning as he took Belle's hand. Their fingers intertwined naturally, like the roots of two old trees that had grown side by side.

"Today was just one of those days where our age seems to catch up with us more than usual. But you know what? That's all right. We're still here, and we're still in love." His eyes met Belle's, and for a moment, they seemed to share an entire conversation without saying a word. She looked back at him with those expressive blue eyes, her silence always speaking volumes.

Belle raised her free hand and began to sign gracefully and deliberately. The news they got today from the Eye Doctor about Jazz's eyesight could have been better. Her hands formed the words, but her eyes conveyed the weight of the news—that he could lose sight one day. Jazz watched her closely, his own eyes betraying a mix of emotions.

"Jazz, my love, I know it was hard to hear," she signed, her fingers trembling ever so slightly. "But that day isn't today. You still have time."

He nodded, swallowing past the lump in his throat. Their cozy living room felt suddenly too small, the clock ticking on the wall a reminder of the sands of time slipping away. Yet, as he looked into Belle's eyes, he found the strength to push aside the fear and hold onto the present.

"Because, as of right now, I can see the faces of everyone I love," Jazz replied, kissing her gently on the forehead. He tasted the salt of her tears, which only heightened the tender sweetness of the moment.

"Promise me something, Belle," he whispered, the words spilling from his heart. "Promise me that we'll make the most of the time we have left, whether it's years or moments."

Her eyes filled with determination and love, Belle nodded firmly. She signed the words he longed to hear with her hands: "I promise, Jazz. We'll make the most of it together."

"Thank you," he breathed, pressing his lips to hers in a gentle, lingering kiss. The world outside their window continued, unaware of the fragile beauty unfolding within. But for Jazz and Belle, that moment held all the promises they could ever need.

"I'm sorry, Dad," Todd replied, relief washing over him. "Always remember that we're here for you, no matter what."

The family sat together, basking in the golden glow of love and connection, ready to face whatever challenges life would bring their way.

Lynn glanced around the room, taking in the unusual stillness that seemed to hang in the air. "Todd was right," she said softly, her gaze falling on her mother. "Something felt... off today. It was like there was quiet tension I couldn't quite put my finger on."

Belle's blue eyes widened, and she exchanged a worried look with Jazz. The two of them had wanted to keep their recent doctor's visit a secret from their children, but it had become increasingly clear that they couldn't hide it any longer.

"Is everything all right now, Mom?" Lynn asked, concern clouding her features. She reached out to squeeze Belle's hand, searching for reassurance in the touch.

Tears welled in Lynn's eyes, and she brushed them away with the back of her hand. "Because we got this together," she agreed fiercely. "We're going to be there for you every step of the way."

"Thank you," Jazz whispered, his voice thick with gratitude and love. A determined glint entered his eyes as he clapped his son's shoulder. "This may be difficult, but we can navigate it together."

Todd leaned forward in his seat, his brow furrowed with concern. "You know, Dad," he began, trying to keep his tone light. When I come home from work and don't see you in the house, I usually know you're across the street having a great time with Belle and Lynn. It makes me want to hurry over and forget about my day, too."

Lynn chimed in, nodding her agreement. "Right. So, when I walked into the house today, it was as quiet as a library. That's not normal for you, even on a bad day." She paused, searching her future father-in-law's eyes. "So, I was like, what's going on?"

Jazz glanced at Belle, who gave him a gentle, encouraging smile. He sighed, rubbing the back of his neck as though the weight of their secret had become too heavy to bear any longer. "We're sorry for trying to keep this from you," he admitted, his voice filled with remorse. "I had some eye issues again today, and Belle suggested we see the doctor."

Jazz took a deep breath, steadying himself as he turned to Belle. Full of love and concern, her blue eyes met his gaze unwaveringly. "As of right now," he said softly, touching her cheek, "enough about me. What about my son and his lovely bride? Because we're not going to have any pity parties in here today because I'm the most blessed man I know, surrounded by so much love."

Lynn blinked away fresh tears, smiling tremulously at Jazz's words. Todd squeezed her hand, and she felt the echo of his resolve to be vital for both their parents. Jazz and Belle had cared for them all their lives; it was time to return that love and support.

"Speaking of brides," Belle signed, her hands moving gracefully to change the topic, "how are the wedding plans coming along?"

Todd and Lynn exchanged a glance, momentarily stunned by the sudden shift in conversation. But they understood – Jazz needed something else to focus on, something happier and more hopeful than the prospect of losing sight.

"Um, well," Lynn began hesitantly, "we've been talking about the ceremony, and Mom mentioned how she'd like me to wear her wedding dress when she married Albert." She looked at Belle, gratitude shining in her eyes.

Belle nodded emphatically, her eyes lighting up with excitement. The room seemed to glow with renewed energy, the airlifting as though a weight had been removed from their shoulders. Jazz watched his beloved's animated signing, and a small smile graced his lips.

"Really?" Todd asked, his voice filled with genuine curiosity. "That's a wonderful idea. I'm sure you'll look amazing in it, Lynn."

"Thank you," she blushed, tucking a strand of blonde hair behind her ear. "It's such an honor. Your mom's dress is beautiful, and I can't think of anything more special than wearing it on our wedding day."

"Sounds perfect," Jazz chimed in, his voice more robust now, the shadows in his eyes retreating as he focused on the joyous event ahead. "And what about the other details? Have you two thought about where you want the ceremony to be?"

"Actually," Todd admitted, sheepishly rubbing the back of his neck, "we've been a bit overwhelmed with everything. Any suggestions from you both would be great."

As they discussed flowers, venues, and guest lists, the living room transformed into a haven of love and shared dreams—a sanctuary from the storm that loomed outside its walls. For a brief moment, Jazz's fading vision seemed like just another challenge they would face together, hand in hand.

In this sacred space, there was no room for fear or pity – only the unshakable bond of family and the strength that came from facing life's trials as one.

"All right," Todd said, trying to keep his voice light as he turned his attention back to the wedding. "We've got the dress settled. How about the music? Any preferences, Dad?"

A slow grin spread across Jazz's face, the twinkle returning to his eyes. "Well, son, I've always been partial to a good jazz band." He chuckled at his pun, the contagious laughter filling the room.

"Jazz it is," Lynn agreed, smiling at her future father-in-law. "I think that would be perfect."

"Great," Todd nodded, glancing at Belle for any further input. "Mom, do you have any ideas for the flowers or decorations?"

"Roses," Belle signed, her hands moving gracefully through the air, Lynn translating for those who couldn't understand. "Red and white roses. They were in my bouquet when I married Albert."

"Red and white roses," Jazz repeated softly, approvingly nodding. "Classic and beautiful, just like you, Belle."

As they continued to discuss the wedding details, Todd could see the light returning to Jazz's eyes, the earlier tension dissipating like morning mist under the sun's warmth. His heart swelled with gratitude for the love and support that filled the room.

"Remember, Todd," Jazz advised with a wink, "the key to a happy marriage is to just say 'yes' to your lovely bride. That way, you'll never go wrong."

The laughter that followed was a balm to their weary souls, and for a moment, the weight of Jazz's diagnosis seemed to lift, replaced by the promise of shared joy and love.

Soon enough, the hour grew late, and Todd knew it was time to take Jazz home for some much-needed rest. As they walked across the street towards their house, the soft glow of the porch light illuminating their path, Todd couldn't help but voice his gratitude.

"Thank you, Dad," he said earnestly and heartfeltly. For everything. I hope to be half the man you are someday—strong, loving, and always there for your family."

Jazz stopped, turning to face his son, the pride in his eyes unmistakable. "Todd, listen to me," he said, his voice thick with emotion. "You've already done more for our family than you know. When I look at you, I see the legacy of Montgomery men, whether through my eyes or the strength of my heart."

As they embraced under the starlit sky, their connection both tangible and unbreakable, Todd knew that no matter what challenges lay ahead, they would face them together, bound by love and the unwavering support of family.

Back in the Thompson's cozy kitchen, Lynn stood beside her mother at the sink, rinsing off the last remnants of dinner from the plates. Her heart swelled with pride as she watched Belle expertly scrubbing each dish. "Mom," Lynn began, her voice soft yet sincere, "I just want you to know how proud I am of you for making those appointments and getting Jazz to the doctor today. You didn't let anything stand in your way, and that's how I know he'll be all right."

Belle paused her washing and looked up at her daughter, her blue eyes shining with love and gratitude. She offered a warm smile before taking a seat at the kitchen table, exhaustion evident in her movements. With her hands, Belle signed, 'I need to sit down because I'm tired. I haven't been that active in a while.' Lynn chuckled gently, her heart full as she continued to wash the dishes.

Meanwhile, Jazz and Todd stepped into their quiet living room across the street. The gentle ticking of the grandfather clock by the door underscored the heaviness between father and son. Feeling a surge of remorse and vulnerability, Jazz turned to Todd, his voice cracking slightly as he spoke.

"Son, I... I need to apologize if I've ever let you down. Despite everything, you've grown into a fine man. And I want you to know how sorry I am if I haven't always been there for you. How should I have?"

Todd looked at his father, seeing the raw emotion in his eyes, and felt a familiar lump forming in his throat. He struggled to find the right words, wanting to reassure Jazz while acknowledging the depth of this moment.

"Jazz, I..." Todd hesitated, searching for the strength to express his feelings fully. "You're my father, and I love you. And I'm grateful for every moment we've shared–the good and difficult times. They've made us who we are today, and I wouldn't trade them for anything."

Jazz's eyes brimmed with tears as he hugged Todd tightly, the two men holding each other in the dimly lit room.

As they stood there, the weight of their shared history and the love that bound them together seemed to fill the space around them.

"Thank you, son," Jazz whispered into Todd's ear, his voice thick with emotion. "I love you, too."

At that moment, despite the challenges ahead, the power of their bond was undeniable—a testament to the resilience of family and the enduring nature of love.

"Jazz, you have nothing to be sorry for," Todd said softly, his voice filled with warmth and genuine affection. "You've been the best role model a son could ever have – every day of my life, I see it in how you treat others, your kindness, and your unwavering love for our family."

The sincerity in Todd's words hung heavy in the air as Jazz looked into his son's eyes, seeing not only the man he had become but also the boy he once was – full of curiosity, laughter, and an endless capacity for love.

"Thank you, Todd," Jazz replied, his voice thick with emotion. "That means more to me than you'll ever know."

As they stood facing each other, the memories began to flow through their minds like a river, carrying them back to happier times when they were all together, united by family bonds.

The past enveloped them, transporting them to a sunny afternoon in the park near their home. Jazz, Belle, Todd, and Lynn sat on a colorful blanket beneath a tall oak tree, its leaves rustling gently in the breeze.

"Look at this, everyone!" Lynn exclaimed, holding up a daisy she had just picked from the grass. With a beaming smile, she turned to her mother and handed it to her. Belle's blue eyes sparkled with delight as she took the flower, her fingers brushing against Lynn's in a silent exchange of affection.

"Let's make a promise," Jazz suggested, his eyes twinkling mischievously. "No matter what happens, we'll always stick together as a family. Through thick and thin, we'll be there for each other."

"Deal!" Todd cried out, raising his hand in the air. The others followed suit, their hands joining a robust, unbreakable circle of love.

"Deal," they all agreed in unison, their voices relentless and filled with hope for the future.

As the memory began to fade, Todd felt the power of their connection again – a reminder that they were never alone, even when faced with adversity. They had each other, and together, they could overcome anything.

"Jazz," he said quietly, his voice steady, "we're going to get through this. We've always been a strong family, which won't change now."

Jazz looked into Todd's eyes, seeing the conviction behind his words, and nodded. "You're right, son. We'll face this together, just like we always have."

With a newfound determination, Todd and Jazz turned to rejoin Belle and Lynn, their hearts lighter and their spirits bolstered by the love that had always bound them together. As they walked side by side, the future seemed a little less daunting because they knew they would face it together as a family.

Jazz paused at the entrance to the living room, his fingers gently tracing the outline of Mary's wedding ring in his pocket. He took a deep breath and stepped inside, where Todd was sitting on the couch, lost in thought.

"Son," Jazz began, his voice soft and tender, "I have something I want to give you."

Todd looked up, his eyes meeting Jazz's as he straightened his seat. "What is it, Dad?"

"Come closer," Jazz said with a warm smile, beckoning him with his hand.

As Todd approached, Jazz pulled the ring from his pocket – a simple gold band that had once belonged to his late wife, Mary. The ring seemed to shimmer in the dim light, a testament to the love they had shared and the life they had built together.

"Your mother would have wanted you to have this," Jazz said, placing the ring in Todd's open palm. "It's her wedding ring. She wore it every day until... well, you know."

Todd stared down at the golden circle in his hand, his eyes filling with tears as memories of his mother flooded his mind. He could still see her vibrant smile, hear her infectious laugh, and feel the warmth of her embrace.

"Thank you," Todd whispered, his voice choked with emotion. "I don't know what to say."

"Mary loved you more than anything in the world," Jazz continued, his eyes glistening. "She would be so proud of the man you've become – of the love and support you've given me and the life you're building with Lynn."

"Mom always believed in us," Todd replied, his voice steady despite the tears streaming down his face. "I wish she could be here to see everything we've accomplished."

"Me too, son, me too," Jazz sighed, placing a hand on Todd's shoulder. "But her spirit lives on in both of us and now, in this ring."

"Is this the legacy you want to pass on to me?" Todd asked, looking earnestly into Jazz's eyes.

"Indeed," Jazz nodded. "The love we shared, the family we created – it's all a part of who you are. And now, it's up to you to carry that legacy."

"Promise me something, Dad," Todd said, his voice wavering.

"Anything, son."

"Promise me that we'll face whatever comes next together – as a family."

Jazz hugged his son tightly, tears streaming down their faces as they clung. "I promise," he whispered, his heart swelling with pride and love for the young man in his arms.

"Thank you," Todd said, pulling away with a determined look in his eyes. "We'll get through this, Dad. Together."

With the ring securely in his hand, Todd felt the weight of his mother's love and the responsibility of carrying on her legacy. He knew they would face challenges ahead, but he was confident they would overcome them – just as they always had – because an unbreakable bond of love and family bound them together.

Chapter 14

T he warm sun cast a golden glow over the little café patio where Todd and Lynn sat with their closest friends, Peter and Sarah. Their laughter floated through the air like a soft melody, mingling with the scent of freshly brewed coffee and the sound of clinking cutlery.

"Okay, okay," Lynn said between giggles, catching her breath. "We have some news to share." She looked at Todd, who nodded in agreement, his eyes sparkling excitedly.

"Go on then," Sarah urged, her blue eyes wide with anticipation.

Todd took a deep breath. "Lynn and I have decided... we're getting married!" He spoke with an uncharacteristic exuberance that made everyone pause momentarily before bursting into surprised congratulations.

"Wait, what?" Peter's jaw dropped, but his eyes were filled with joy. "I didn't even know you two were at that point!"

"Neither did we," Lynn admitted, "until recently. We've been spending so much time together caring for our parents, and one day it just clicked."

Todd interjected, his voice softer now, "We realized that life is unpredictable, and time is precious. We refuse to waste any more of it apart from each other."

Sarah dabbed at her eyes with a napkin, clearly moved by the couple's sincerity. "That's beautiful. We're so happy for you both."

"Thank you," Todd said, squeezing Lynn's hand under the table. "Now, we have another favor to ask. Peter, will you be my best man?"

"And Sarah," Lynn said, "will you be my maid of honor?"

"Of course!" they replied in unison.

Later that afternoon, Todd and Lynn strolled hand-in-hand through the picturesque park, the leaves above them rustling gently in the breeze. They found a quiet bench overlooking a pond, its surface shimmering like a mirror, reflecting the day's beauty.

"Okay, so what's next with this wedding planning?" Todd asked, his brow furrowed in thought.

Lynn took a small notebook and pen from her purse. "First, let's consider possible venues."

"Right," Todd agreed. "What about the community center? It's big enough to hold everyone, and we could easily transform it into something magical."

"Perfect," Lynn smiled, jotting down the idea. "Now, decorations." She tapped her pen against her chin, thinking. "I've always loved the idea of twinkling lights and soft pastel colors."

"Sounds lovely," Todd said, the corners of his eyes crinkling as he imagined their special day. "And the guest list? We should keep it simple – just family and close friends."

"Agreed," Lynn nodded, beginning to write down names. "This is happening, isn't it?"

Todd leaned in and placed a gentle kiss on her forehead. "Yes, it is. And I couldn't be happier."

As they continued their planning, surrounded by the park's serene beauty, Todd and Lynn reveled in the knowledge that they were building a future together – one filled with love, laughter, and the unwavering support of those who mattered most.

Lynn's fingers danced lightly over the screen of her phone, composing a message to her mother and Jazz. The sunlight filtered through the leaves overhead, casting dappled shadows on her face as she typed excitedly.

"Mom, Jazz, we're at the park planning our wedding. Would you like to join us? Your input would mean the world to us. Love, Lynn."

Her heart swelled with anticipation as she hit send and glanced over at Todd, who was lost in thought, sketching out possible seating arrangements on paper. She hoped their parents would be thrilled to help plan this special day.

"Message sent," she said softly, catching Todd's eye and sharing a smile that conveyed their joy.

"Great. I know they'll be excited to help," he replied, his voice warm and comforting.

Minutes later, Lynn felt her phone buzz, signaling an incoming message. She quickly opened it to find her mother's response.

"Dearest Lynn, We are overjoyed and on our way! Love, Belle."

"Mom and Jazz are coming," Lynn informed Todd, her eyes sparkling with happiness. "Let's make some room for them."

Together, they shifted their belongings, creating a welcoming space on the soft grass. The scent of nearby roses filled the air, adding to the idyllic atmosphere of their impromptu planning session.

"Here they come!" Todd exclaimed, spotting the familiar silhouettes of Belle and Jazz making their way toward them.

"Hey, you two lovebirds!" Jazz called out, grinning from ear to ear. Though his vision had been fading in recent years, the warmth in his voice betrayed the happiness he felt in his heart.

"Hello, dear ones," Belle signed gracefully, her expressive blue eyes meeting Lynn's as she drew closer.

"Hi, Mom. Hi, Jazz," Lynn greeted them, her voice thick with emotion. "We're so glad you could join us."

"Wouldn't miss it for the world," Jazz said, kneeling beside Todd and clapping his hand on his shoulder.

"Your father's right," Belle signed, her eyes shining with love. "We're here to help in any way we can."

"Thank you," Lynn replied, grateful for their support. "We've been discussing venues, decorations, and the guest list. We think the community center would be perfect, but we need your ideas and input."

"Of course!" Jazz exclaimed, his enthusiasm contagious. "Let's get started!"

As they delved into the details of planning the wedding, Lynn felt a profound sense of gratitude wash over her. This day was not just about her and Todd; it was about intertwining two families bound together by love and understanding. As the sun dipped lower in the sky, casting a warm glow over their gathering, she knew that this moment – surrounded by those who mattered most – was a memory she would cherish forever.

The sun shone brightly, casting playful shadows on the cobblestone streets as the town buzzed with a new-found sense of purpose. Neighbors exchanged knowing smiles and warm words of encouragement as they worked together to transform the community center for Todd and Lynn's wedding.

"Hey, Ms. Thompson! We're here to help!" called out a young boy from down the street, his arms full of colorful flowers. Lynn smiled warmly, touched by the town's unwavering support.

"Thank you, Tommy," she replied, taking the flowers from him and placing them on a table nearby.

Across the room, Jazz moved a ladder into position while Todd hung twinkling lights from the rafters. Belle, her hands busy arranging flowers into stunning bouquets, looked up and signed, "Todd, you need to take a break. You two need to choose your wedding cake flavors at the bakery."

"Good idea! We've been meaning to do that," Todd agreed, wiping beads of sweat from his brow. He turned to Lynn, her cheeks flushed with excitement. "Ready?"

"Absolutely," she said, linking her arm with his as they walked hand-in-hand toward the local bakery.

Upon entering the bakery, the couple was enveloped by the sweet aroma of freshly baked pastries. An array of cakes lined the display case, their intricate designs beckoning them closer.

"Welcome, Todd and Lynn! We've been expecting you," the baker, Mrs. Thompson, cheerfully greeted them. I've prepared a variety of flavors for you to taste."

"Thank you, Mrs. Thompson," Lynn said, her eyes widening as she took in the assortment of miniature cakes before them.

As they sampled each delicate flavor – rich chocolate ganache, tangy lemon, and velvety red velvet – their thoughts drifted back to memories of shared desserts and stolen moments in each other's arms.

"Remember that evening by the lake?" Todd asked, a playful glint in his eyes as he took a bite of the raspberry-filled cake.

Lynn blushed, recalling the tender touch of his hand as they fed each other beneath the moonlit sky. "How could I forget?"

"Ah, lovebirds," Mrs. Thompson said, smiling warmly at their connection. "What's your favorite so far?"

"The raspberry," Lynn replied, her eyes sparkling with certainty.

"I agree," Todd said, gently squeezing Lynn's hand. "It reminds us of something special."

"Raspberry it is, then!" Mrs. Thompson exclaimed, making a note on her order pad. "I'll make sure your wedding cake is just perfect."

"Thank you," Todd said, gratitude evident in his voice.

As they left the bakery arm-in-arm, the weight of their decision seemed to lift from their shoulders. The town had come together to support them, and now, their wedding felt more accurate.

"Everyone's been so incredible," Lynn mused, leaning into Todd's embrace. "It's like our love has brought the whole town closer."

"Love has a way of doing that," Todd whispered, kissing her forehead tenderly. "And ours is just beginning."

Lynn and Belle stood in the bridal boutique, surrounded by a sea of white gowns, each more intricate than the last. The room was filled with hushed whispers from other brides-to-be and their entourages as they excitedly discussed the merits of lace and tulle. Lynn glanced over at her mother, who offered an encouraging smile, her blue eyes shining brightly.

"All right," Lynn said, taking a deep breath. "Let's try some on."

As Lynn slipped into one dress after another, she grew increasingly disheartened. None of them felt quite right—the fabric was too heavy, the embellishments too ostentatious. Belle watched her daughter's frustration mount, her heart aching for her.

"None of these dresses are me," Lynn sighed, her voice tinged with disappointment. "What if I can't find the perfect one?"

Belle reached out to touch her daughter's hand, her gaze full of empathy. She closed her eyes briefly, then nodded at the wedding dressmaker. The dressmaker disappeared into a back room, emerging moments later with a garment bag draped over her arm.

"Your mother wanted me to keep this as a surprise," the dressmaker said softly, unzipping the bag to reveal a beautiful gown. "She had it altered just for you."

Lynn stared at the dress, her breath catching in her throat. It was her mother's wedding dress, transformed for her – delicate lace sleeves added, a sweeping train that would float behind her as she walked down the aisle. Tears welled up in her eyes as she realized the significance of the gift.

"Mom... I don't know what to say," Lynn stammered, her voice thick with emotion. Belle smiled, her eyes brimming with her tears, as they shared a moment that transcended the need for words.

Across town, Todd and Jazz navigated through rows of suits in every shade of gray and blue. Jazz, his vision blurred by the progression of his eyesight loss, relied on touch to discern between fabrics while Todd carefully considered each option.

"Remember, son," Jazz said with a playful grin, "this is the suit you'll be wearing when you say 'I do.' No pressure."

"Hilarious, Dad," Todd replied, rolling his eyes good-naturedly. Despite his sarcasm, he felt grateful for his father's support and fun.

"Hey, how about this one?" Todd asked, holding a three-piece navy suit with a subtle pinstripe pattern.

"Feels nice," Jazz said, fingers over the fabric. "But I think we can find something even better."

As they continued their search, Todd couldn't help but feel a sense of camaraderie with his father. The shared experience of preparing for his wedding softened the rough edges of their relationship, allowing them both to appreciate the simple joy of being together.

"Okay, what about this one?" Todd asked, presenting a charcoal gray suit with impeccable tailoring. Jazz touched the fabric, his face breaking into a broad smile.

"Perfect," he declared. "The right balance of elegance and comfort."

"Then it's the one," Todd said, relief washing over him. As they stood side-by-side in the fitting room mirror, the reflection of their bond was clear as day, and a quiet understanding passed between father and son – a promise to cherish the love and family they had found in each other.

The morning sun beamed through the glass windows of the community center, casting its warm golden glow on the vibrant decorations that adorned the room. Delicate garlands of flowers intertwined with twinkling fairy lights draped from the ceiling, creating a magical canopy above the guests' heads. The air was filled with anticipation and excitement as the townspeople, dressed in their finest attire, chatted animatedly while they took their seats.

Belle stood at the entrance, her silver hair pinned back elegantly, her expressive blue eyes taking in every detail of the transformed space. She felt Lynn's hand gently squeeze her own, a silent communication of gratitude and love shared between mother and daughter.

"Mom, it's perfect," Lynn whispered, her voice choked with emotion. Belle nodded, a warm smile lighting up her face as she squeezed her daughter's hand.

Jazz walked over to join them, his arm linked around Todd's. He could sense the room's beauty even if his eyesight didn't allow him to see all the fine details. "Everyone's here," he said softly, somehow able to detect the presence of the gathered friends and family. "This is going to be a day we'll never forget."

As they mingled with the guests, an elegantly dressed woman approached Belle and Jazz, her face a mixture of surprise and nostalgia. "Belle? Jazz?" she asked tentatively, searching their faces for recognition. "It's me, Martha."

A flicker of recognition lit up Belle's eyes, and she touched Martha's arm. Jazz offered her a warm smile, sensing the history between the women. "Martha, it has been a long time," he said kindly.

"Too long," Martha agreed, tears welling in her eyes. "I saw you two standing there, still so much in love after fifty years, and I just had to come over. I need to apologize."

"Apologize for what?" Jazz asked, genuinely puzzled.

"Jazz, I was the one who drove Belle to the train platform when you left for the military," Martha confessed, her voice cracking. "I thought if you cared, you would have stayed."

"Ah, I see," Jazz said, his tone gentle and understanding. He looked at Belle, her eyes filled with memories of that long-ago day. "Well, Martha, no apology is needed. You see, love is undefeated. Sometimes, we do not determine the path, but this is evidence that this wasn't up to us. Belle and I had another chapter to finish and had to cross paths again."

Tears streamed down Martha's cheeks as she listened to Jazz's wise words. She glanced at Todd and others waiting for the wedding, their love and happiness shining brightly on this special day. "Thank you, Jazz," she whispered. "You're right. Love never loses."

As they made their way towards the front of the room, Belle and Jazz could feel the love surrounding them—from their children, friends, and the entire community. As they stood side by side, hand in hand, they knew that love would carry them through the rest of their lives, always guiding them back to each other, no matter the twists and turns along the way.

The ceremony began with a hush as if the air held its breath in anticipation. Todd stood at the altar, his hands fidgeting with the hem of his jacket, eyes locked on the community center entrance where Lynn would soon appear. The room was bathed in the soft, warm glow of twinkling lights that illuminated the colorful decorations with a touch of enchantment.

"Are you ready?" Jazz whispered, his hand resting reassuringly on his son's shoulder.

Todd swallowed hard, his chest tightening with nerves and joy. "I've never been more ready for anything in my life," he replied, barely audible.

As the music swelled, the doors opened to reveal Lynn, her radiant smile eclipsing the beauty of her flowing white gown. Todd's breath caught in his throat, his heart swelling with love and gratitude as she approached him, arm in arm with her mother, Belle.

"Friends and loved ones," the officiant began, "we are gathered here today to celebrate the union of Todd and Lynn in holy matrimony." He paused, allowing the couple to take each other's hands before continuing, "Now, they will share their vows."

"From the moment we met," Todd began, his voice wavering with raw emotion, "I knew there was something special about you. You have shown me what it means to love and be loved truly, and I promise to cherish and support you for the rest of our lives."

Lynn's eyes shimmered with tears as she squeezed Todd's hands. "Todd, you have been my rock and refuge when times were tough. Your love has made me stronger, and I vow to stand by your side through thick and thin, cherishing every moment we have together."

As they exchanged rings, sealing their promises with a symbol of eternity, the room fell silent once more, holding its collective breath for the moment that would unite them forever. Just as the officiant prepared to pronounce them husband and wife, a sound filled the room – a sound no one expected.

Lynn stood before the small gathering, her gaze unwavering as she locked eyes with her new husband. The glow of the candles flickered around them, casting a warm light across their faces and reflecting in the tears that threatened to spill down her cheeks. With a deep breath, she opened her mouth and began to sing, her voice trembling slightly but filled with the love that swelled within her heart.

"Love is a journey," she sang, each word carrying the weight of her mother's wisdom and love. As the song flowed from her lips, it was as if the very air around them hummed with energy, radiating love and devotion.

"Finding the courage to open your heart to someone else," Lynn continued, her voice steady and clear, "and the transformative power of a love that could span life."

As the song echoed through the room, Todd felt a shiver run down his spine, his heart swelling with emotion. The sincerity in her voice and the depth of feeling conveyed by those simple words touched him deeply. Watching her sing, he found himself lost in her eyes, the same warm smile that had first drawn him to her now shining brightly for all to see.

"Did you feel that?" whispered one of the guests, her voice barely audible over Lynn's singing. "It's like... pure love."

"Her mother wrote that song just for this day," another guest murmured, wiping a tear.

For a moment, the world seemed to fall away, leaving only the two of them standing together, surrounded by the love of their family and friends. In this instant, Todd knew, without a doubt, that their love was destined to guide them through whatever challenges they would face in the years to come.

As Lynn finished the song, she stepped toward her mother, her eyes glistening with unshed tears. She wrapped her arms around the older woman, whispering words of gratitude and love that only they could hear.

"Thank you, Mom," Lynn whispered, her voice thick with emotion. "I couldn't have asked for a more perfect gift."

As they pulled apart from their embrace, Lynn looked back at Todd, who stood there with his heart overflowing with love for her and her family. At this moment, their story was beginning, and it was a story filled with the beauty of life and the connections they would forge together.

The sun dipped low in the sky, casting a warm golden glow over the reception area. Laughter echoed through the air as friends and family gathered around tables adorned with delicate flowers and flickering candles. The scent of freshly baked bread and savory dishes wafted from the buffet, tempting guests to indulge in the delicious spread.

"First, I want to say thank you all for sharing this special day with us," Todd began, raising his glass high. The tinkling of silverware against crystal rang out in unison as everyone followed suit. "To the love of my life, Lynn, who has taught me what it means to cherish each moment we have together truly." He paused, smiling at his bride, her eyes brimming with tears of happiness. "And to Jazz and Belle, who have shown us that love transcends time and every obstacle life throws our way."

"Here, here!" someone called out from the crowd, and the guests cheered as they toasted to the newlyweds. As the clinking of glasses subsided, lively music began to fill the air, inviting couples young and old to dance beneath the twinkling string lights that crisscrossed overhead.

Jazz stood up, his eyes shining with pride. Even though his vision was fading, he could still make out the silhouettes of his daughter and new son-in-law on the dance floor, their love radiating like the sun. He turned to Belle, her blue eyes sparkling with joy as she watched their family grow.

"May I have this dance, my love?" Jazz asked, extending his hand to Belle. She smiled warmly, placing her hand in his as she nodded in agreement. Together, they stepped onto the dance floor, swaying gently to the rhythm of the music.

As they danced, Jazz could feel the weight of their shared history in each step – the years spent apart, the longing that had filled their hearts, and the second chance they'd been given to reunite. And now, as they danced together, it was as if all those years apart were nothing more than a blip in the timeline of their love.

"Can you believe our kids are married to each other?" Jazz whispered into Belle's ear, his breath warm against her skin. Belle shook her head, her eyes glistening with unshed tears. She squeezed Jazz's hand tighter, grateful for this moment they could share, surrounded by the love of their family and friends.

"Thank you," Belle mouthed, her eyes locked on Jazz's. He knew what she meant – thank you for returning to her, never giving up on their love, and showing her that sometimes life's detours only lead us right back to where we belong.

As the music continued and laughter bubbled around them, Jazz and Belle continued to dance, lost in each other's embrace. The world seemed to fade away, leaving only the two dancing beneath the stars, their love a beacon guiding them through the night. And as they danced, they knew that no matter the twists and turns life might throw, their love would always remain strong, unwavering, and undefeated.

The dance floor was alive with movement, the townsfolk swirling around Jazz and Belle like vibrant colors in a kaleidoscope. Todd and Lynn glided through the crowd, their laughter contagious as they reveled in the joy of their new beginning.

"Isn't this amazing?" Lynn exclaimed, her eyes sparkling excitedly as she looked up at Todd. He grinned, his grip on her waist tightening ever so slightly.

"Absolutely," he agreed, the warmth in his voice evident. "Seeing everyone come together like this... it's incredible."

As they danced, the music seemed to reach every corner of the room, inviting even the most reserved of guests – including Ray and Maggie – to join in the celebration. The two hesitated momentarily before taking each other's hand and stepping onto the dance floor.

"Come on, Ray!" Maggie called out over the music. "Don't let these old bones hold you back now."

"Who's got old bones?" Ray retorted playfully, twirling Maggie with surprising grace. Their laughter filled the air, adding to the jubilant atmosphere that enveloped the room.

Across the dance floor, Sam clapped her hands in delight as Tom spun her around. Her infectious laughter caught the attention of those nearby, and soon enough, a small group had formed around them, eager to share in the joy.

As Todd and Lynn continued to dance, they couldn't help but notice the happiness that radiated from everyone around them. It was as if the entire town had been lifted by the power of love, proving once again that it could conquer all.

"Look at them," Todd whispered, nodding towards his parents. Jazz held Belle close, his face full of adoration as he guided her gently across the dance floor. Despite his failing eyesight, he seemed to see nothing but her.

"I know," Lynn replied softly, her heart swelling with affection. "It's beautiful, isn't it?"

"More than you know," Todd said, his gaze never leaving their parents as they danced. At that moment, he was struck by a profound realization: their love had healed old wounds and inspired the entire town to celebrate.

"Love is undefeated," Lynn mused, echoing the sentiment Jazz had shared earlier. Todd smiled and pulled her closer, his heart brimming with gratitude for the woman who had shown him that love could simultaneously be simple and extraordinary.

"Let's make a promise," he said, his voice barely audible above the music. "No matter what life throws at us, we'll face it together, hand in hand, just like them."

"Deal," Lynn whispered, sealing their vow with a tender kiss as the dance floor spun around them.

And so, as the night wore on and the stars shone brightly overhead, the people of this small town danced – not only in celebration of Todd and Lynn's love but also as a testament to the enduring power of love itself. For in their hearts, they knew that even when faced with adversity, love would always find a way to triumph, bringing joy and new beginnings to all those who dared to believe in its magic.

Chapter 15

The sun cast a golden hue upon the park as Jazz and Belle strolled hand in hand beneath the sprawling canopy of trees. Dewdrops on blades of grass shimmered like tiny diamonds, and birds sang their morning melodies. Jazz's heart swelled with love for Belle, her silver hair dancing in the breeze. He squeezed her hand gently as they walked, and she returned the gesture warmly.

"Remember when we first came here?" Jazz asked, his voice tender and nostalgic. His eyesight was fading, but his memories were vivid. We were just kids, running around without a care in the world."

Belle nodded, her blue eyes shining with the recollection. She pointed toward an old oak tree near the pond's edge, where they had once carved their initials into its bark. Jazz chuckled, recalling how they had spent countless hours by that tree, lost in each other's company.

"Time sure flies, doesn't it?" Jazz mused, looking at their reflection in the pond. Their faces may have aged, but their love remained as strong as ever.

Jazz noticed a familiar scent drifting through the air as they strolled. He inhaled deeply, savoring the aroma of freshly baked goods from their favorite bakery just around the corner.

"Shall we stop for a treat, my dear?" he suggested, his mouth-watering.

Belle's eyes lit up, and she nodded enthusiastically. They entered the quaint bakery, greeted by the smiling face of the baker who had known them for years. The glass display case was filled with various delicious pastries, their flavors so tempting that it was nearly impossible to choose just one.

"Two raspberry tarts, please," Jazz said, knowing Belle's fondness for the sweet and tangy dessert. The baker carefully placed the tarts in a small box, tied them with a ribbon, and handed it to Jazz.

"Enjoy," the baker said warmly. "You two always remind me of what true love looks like."

As they settled on a nearby bench in the park, Jazz carefully opened the box, revealing the delicious treats within. The tarts' flaky crusts and vibrant red raspberries were as enticing as ever, and he couldn't help but smile at Belle's wide-eyed excitement.

"Here you go, my love," Jazz said, handing her a tart. He watched as she took a bite, her eyes closing in delight as she savored the flavors. Jazz took his bite, allowing the taste to linger on his tongue—a sweet reminder of their lifelong romance.

"Every time I eat one of these, it takes me back to the first time we tried these tarts," Jazz mused, his voice filled with affection. "I still remember how your face lit up when you tasted it for the first time."

Belle nodded, her eyes glistening with unspoken memories. She touched Jazz's cheek gently, conveying more than words ever could. At that moment, they realize they never had the opportunity to be husband and wife, but their love had weathered life's storms together and had emerged stronger.

With every bite, they cherished the simple pleasure of sharing a sweet treat, surrounded by the park's beauty, where their love had blossomed. Hand in hand, they walked towards their future, hearts overflowing with the precious gift of each other's company.

A warm breeze rustled through the leaves of the surrounding trees, carrying with it the sweet scent of honeysuckle. Jazz closed his eyes momentarily, relishing the familiar weight of Belle's head resting on his shoulder.

"Remember that time we went camping in the mountains?" Jazz asked, his voice soft and filled with nostalgia. "We were so young and naive, thinking we could conquer any challenge nature threw us."

Belle chuckled silently, her body shaking against his. She nodded her head, her blue eyes sparkling with the memory. Her hand gestured upwards, mimicking the towering peaks they had once climbed together.

"Those stars... I'll never forget how many there were or how bright they shone," Jazz continued, his eyes focused on the clear sky above them. "And neither of us could start a fire to save our lives. We must have spent hours gathering twigs and trying to ignite them."

With a playful smile, Belle tapped Jazz's arm and held two crossed fingers, indicating a failed attempt.

"Ah, yes, you're right," he laughed heartily. "It was you who finally got the fire going. You always did have a knack for finding solutions when we needed them most."

Belle blushed and squeezed his hand, memories of that adventure flooding back. The way they huddled together for warmth, their laughter echoing through the vast forest, and the bond they forged under those starlit skies.

"Speaking of memories," Jazz said, shifting slightly to reach behind him. "I have something special for you." He pulled out a worn, leather-bound photo album, its pages thick with memories from their earliest days together.

Belle's eyes widened in surprise, and her hands flew to her mouth as a tear escaped the corner of her eye. She looked up at Jazz, her gratitude shining through her gaze.

"Open it, my love," he whispered, gently placing the album in her lap. "Let's take a trip down memory lane together."

Belle slowly opened the cover, revealing the first photo of them as teenagers, their smiles bright and their eyes filled with the anticipation of a lifetime spent side by side. As the pages turned one after the other, they wandered through their shared history, each photograph a glimpse into the love that had bound their souls together.

At that moment, time they stood still for Jazz and Belle. As they rocked back and forth on the porch swing, their laughter and tears mingling like drops of rain in a summer storm, they were reminded of their incredible journey together. And though challenges lay ahead, they knew they would face them hand in hand, hearts forever entwined.

The sun dipped low in the sky, casting long shadows across Jazz and Belle as they pored over the photo album's pages. Belle's fingers traced the creased edges of a photograph that captured their first anniversary. In the image, she wore a simple white sundress, her silver hair cascading down her back, while Jazz donned his favorite gray suit and a boyish grin.

"Remember this?" Jazz asked with a chuckle, his eyes crinkling at the corners. "I was so nervous about making dinner for you that night."

Belle nodded, her eyes sparkling with amusement. She tapped the picture gently before pointing towards the kitchen, suggesting they recreate that long-ago meal together.

"Ah, I see what you're getting at," Jazz said, grinning broadly. "A romantic candlelit dinner, just like old times. Let's do it."

Together, they rose from the porch swing, hands intertwined, and made their way into the inviting warmth of the kitchen. As the music played softly in the background, they began preparing their favorite dishes, their movements perfectly synchronized after decades spent side by side.

With careful precision, Jazz sliced through ripe tomatoes, their vibrant red juices staining the cutting board. Belle, her slender fingers deftly working, chopped onions and garlic, the fragrant aromas mingling with the savory scent of the searing steak that sizzled on the stove.

"Be careful with those onions, love," Jazz warned, squinting as he tried to focus on the chopping. "My eyes might not be what they used to be, but I still know when you're up to something."

Belle smirked and shook her head, her eyes twinkling with mischief as she continued to work. She reached out, touching Jazz's arm reassuringly, and he smiled in response, heartened by the familiar comfort of her touch.

As the sky outside the window turned from a brilliant orange to a deep, velvety blue, they lit candles and filled their plates, the soft glow of the flickering flames casting a warm, intimate ambiance over the scene.

"Cheers to us," Jazz whispered, holding his wine glass in a toast. Belle clinked her own against his, their eyes locked in a silent exchange of love and gratitude.

They sat at the small, round table, bathed in candlelight, and began savoring each bite of their lovingly prepared meal. The flavors of their youth danced on their tongues, a culinary journey back in time that brought forth sweet and bittersweet memories.

"Who would have thought we'd be here, doing this again after all these years?" Jazz mused, the wonderment evident in his voice. "It's like fate conspired to bring us back together."

Belle nodded, her eyes filled with warmth and affection. She reached across the table, placing her hand atop Jazz's and giving it a gentle squeeze. Their unspoken connection resonated deeply within them, a testament to the strength and resilience of their love.

As evening settled around them, Jazz and Belle remained lost in their world of memories, their hearts intertwined as tightly as their hands across the table. They had weathered many storms throughout their lives, but now – surrounded by the soft glow of candlelight and the echoes of their shared history – they found solace and contentment in each other's company. And as the stars twinkled above them, mirroring the light in their eyes, they knew they were exactly where they were meant to be.

As they finished their meal, Jazz rose from the table and walked to the living room, extending his hand towards Belle. Her eyes lit up as she recognized the gesture, a memory of their youth coming to life at that moment. She took his hand and stepped onto the worn wooden floor together.

"Remember our first dance?" Jazz asked, his voice low and tender as he guided Belle gently into position. "I was so nervous, I nearly tripped over my feet."

Belle's smile widened, her eyes sparkling with amusement as she recalled the memory. She nodded, placing her hand on his shoulder while her other held his tightly. They began to sway slowly, their bodies finding the familiar rhythm they had once shared. The soft melody of their favorite song filled the room, transporting them back to those early days of young love.

"Did you ever think we would be here, dancing together like this again?" Jazz whispered, his eyes searching hers for an answer.

Belle shook her head, her heart swelling with gratitude as she leaned closer. Their bodies moved in perfect harmony, attuned to each other's every breath and heartbeat. The fifty years from the past were gone, leaving only the connection between two souls who had found their way back.

The song ended, but neither Jazz nor Belle wanted to break the spell. As they stood there, lost in each other's embrace, Jazz reached into his pocket and pulled out a small, folded piece of paper. With a deep breath, he handed it to Belle.

"Before my eyesight gets any worse, I wanted to write you something special," he explained, his voice trembling with vulnerability. "I hope you can feel the love behind each word on the paper."

Belle unfolded the paper carefully, her eyes scanning the lines of Jazz's shaky handwriting. Tears welled in her eyes as she read his heartfelt words, the depth of his love and gratitude for their second chance at life together spilling across the page. She looked up at him, her eyes glistening with unshed tears, and pressed the letter to her chest, a silent gesture of appreciation.

"Thank you," she mouthed, her eyes never leaving his.

Jazz reached out and brushed away a single tear that had escaped down Belle's cheek. "You're my world, Belle," he whispered, pulling her close again, their hearts beating. "I wouldn't trade this - any of it - for anything."

As they held each other close, the warmth of their love enveloped them, wrapping them in a cocoon of tenderness that transcended time and space. At that moment, they understood that their love was a rare and precious gift that would carry them through every challenge and hardship that life could throw. Jazz and Belle knew they were home as they continued dancing beneath the evening light's soft glow.

Belle's eyes shimmered with the last light of day as she reached out to take Jazz's hand, her fingers delicate yet firm in their grip. The warmth from his palm seemed to melt away the chill of the evening air.

"Come with me," she mouthed, a soft smile gracing her lips.

"Where are we going?" Jazz asked, curiosity dancing in his voice.

"Outside," she gestured towards the backyard, her eyes sparkling like the stars above.

As they stepped into the dew-kissed grass, Jazz felt a sense of serenity wash over him. The night sky had donned its velvet cloak embroidered with diamond stars. Belle released his hand momentarily, only to return it with a small paper lantern.

"Are we..." Jazz trailed off, his heart swelling with emotion.

"Let's release them together," Belle communicated with her eyes, a tender smile.

Jazz nodded his throat tight with gratitude. They lit the lanterns with practiced hands, watching the flame flicker and dance within. As the lanterns filled with warm air, they swayed gently, urging them to let go.

"Ready?" Jazz whispered, his eyes meeting Belle's.

She nodded, her blue eyes reflecting the fire's glow. Together, they released the lanterns, watching as they rose into the night sky. The orange orbs danced among the stars, symbolizing their hopes and dreams - fulfilled and those yet to come.

"Thank you, Belle," Jazz murmured, his voice barely audible over the rustling leaves. "I've always dreamed of doing this with you."

"Me too," she mouthed, her gaze never leaving their floating wishes.

As the lanterns disappeared into the darkness, they returned to the porch swing, a cozy blanket draped across its wooden frame. Jazz held it open for Belle, who settled in beside him. Wrapping the blanket around them, they nestled close, their breaths mingling in the cool night air.

"Jazz?" Belle mouthed, her eyes searching his face.

"Yes, my love?"

"Promise me," she paused, her fingers tracing circles on his arm, "promise me we'll never forget these moments."

Jazz's heart ached with tenderness as he pressed his forehead to hers. "I promise, Belle. Every memory, every moment, they're etched into my soul. They're a part of us."

"Good," she mouthed, a tear rolling down her cheek. Jazz brushed it away gently, his fingers lingering on her soft skin. As they sat there, wrapped in each other's arms and the blanket's warmth, they gazed at the stars—those eternal witnesses to their love.

"Sweet dreams, Belle," Jazz whispered, kissing her forehead tenderly.

"Sweet dreams," she mouthed back, her eyes drifting shut. She knew their love would continue to burn like the brightest star, guiding them through the darkest nights and into the light of a new day.

The night sky swirled above Jazz and Belle as they remained nestled in the porch swing, the constellation of their love painted across the heavens. They breathed in sync; each exhaled a silent whisper shared between their souls.

"Jazz?" Belle mouthed, her eyes reflecting the shimmering stars above them.

"Right here, my love," he whispered, gently squeezing her hand.

"Thank you," she mouthed, her fingers brushing his cheek. He could feel her gratitude through her touch, like a warm breeze on a summer evening.

"Always, Belle. You're my world," he said, the words escaping his heart like fireflies illuminating the night. Her smile bloomed like the moon's glow, casting a spell of serenity around them.

As the night deepened, so did their embrace. Their breaths slowed, lulled by the songs of crickets and the promise of forever. Eventually, sleep found them, wrapping its arms around them as they slumbered peacefully in each other's arms.

The first golden rays of sunlight peeked through the trees, painting the landscape with hues of pink and orange. The chorus of birdsong filled the air, punctuating the dawn with melodies of life and love.

As the sun rose higher, its warm embrace stretched through the windows of Todd and Lynn's bedroom. The golden light illuminated the room, casting a warm glow over the pair as they lay entwined beneath the soft sheets.

"Morning," Todd whispered into Lynn's ear, his breath tickling her neck.

"Good morning," she replied, her voice still heavy with sleep.

"Stay here," he instructed gently, disentangling himself from her embrace and padding softly out of the room.

A tantalizing aroma soon wafted in from the kitchen, enticing Lynn to rise from the comfort of her bed. Before she could fully awaken, Todd returned to the room, bearing a tray laden with steaming pancakes, fresh fruit, and a cup of coffee.

"Surprise," he said, his eyes twinkling with affection.

"Breakfast in bed?" Lynn asked, her heart swelling with gratitude. "You're too good to me."

Todd set the tray on the bed, and they kissed tenderly before settling back against the pillows to enjoy their meal. Each bite of the fluffy pancake brought a sense of contentment, as if the flavors were woven with love.

"Something feels different today," Lynn mused between bites. "Like there's magic in the air."

"Maybe it's just the love we're all feeling," Todd suggested, sipping his coffee.

"Or maybe it's Jazz and Belle," Lynn said thoughtfully. "Their love seems to have a life of its own, doesn't it?"

"Speaking of which, we should find them and share this moment," she proposed, her eyes sparkling with excitement.

"Agreed," Todd nodded, his heart feeling lighter at the prospect of sharing this happiness with his father and Belle.

With newfound energy, they quickly finished their breakfast and ventured outside, hand in hand, searching for their loved ones. As they stepped into the sunlit morning, a sense of warmth and gratitude enveloped them, intertwining their hearts with the love that Jazz and Belle had found in each other.

"Let's find them," Lynn said softly, her voice filled with anticipation and joy.

"Let's make today unforgettable," Todd agreed, his heart swelling with love for Lynn, his father, and Belle.

Together, they wandered through the sun-dappled garden, following the sweet sound of birdsong and the gentle rustle of leaves as they sought out Jazz and Belle, eager to share this moment of pure, unadulterated love.

Todd and Lynn wandered through the garden in search of Jazz and Belle. Their laughter filled the air as they recalled a day they had all spent together, creating new memories that would forever be etched in their hearts.

"Remember when Dad tried to teach us all how to fish?" Todd chuckled at the memory, his eyes crinkling with amusement. "I've never seen so many tangled fishing lines, and Belle just sat there, watching us struggle."

"Until she calmly reached over, untangled all the knots, and caught the first fish within minutes!" Lynn laughed, her hand instinctively resting on her heart, feeling the warmth of the memory.

"Mom's always had this grace about her," Lynn continued, her voice softening. "It's no wonder Dad fell for her. They bring out the best in each other."

"True," Todd agreed, a wistful smile playing on his lips as he thought about his father's love for Belle. He could see it in how Jazz spoke to her, never raising his voice, always listening intently despite her inability to speak. And it was evident in the way Belle's eyes lit up whenever Jazz was near, a silent language only the two understood.

"Let's check the porch swing," Lynn suggested, pulling Todd from his reverie. "They love spending time there."

As they rounded the corner of the house, hand in hand, they saw Jazz and Belle nestled together on the wooden swing, wrapped in a cozy blanket. The sun cast a warm glow upon their serene faces, belying that both their souls had quietly slipped away during the night.

Todd felt his breath catch in his throat while tears rose in Lynn's eyes. The sight before them was heartbreaking yet undeniably beautiful - two souls intertwined, bound by love until their last breath.

"Look how peaceful they are," Lynn whispered, her voice trembling.

"Moments like these make me realize how precious life is," Todd murmured, his eyes never leaving the sight of his father and Belle. "They were lucky to have each other."

"Jazz and Belle taught us that love transcends time, age, and even words," Lynn added, her tears falling freely. "Their love was a gift we all got to witness."

"Let's cherish their memory," Todd said softly, wiping away a tear of his own. "We'll remember them as they were, two souls in love, bound together by a promise to live life to the fullest."

With hearts heavy yet filled with gratitude, Todd and Lynn stood hand in hand, honoring Jazz and Belle's love. This was a testament to the beauty and power of authentic, everlasting devotion.

Chapter 16
Epilogue

A gentle breeze rustled the vibrant blooms of roses and lilies that adorned the small, white gazebo in the town square. The sun cast a warm, golden glow on the gathered crowd, their hushed murmurs mingling with the soft chirping of birds. Todd stood beside Lynn, each wearing a somber expression as they held hands, feeling the weight of grief and pride in equal measure.

"Jazz and Belle truly brought this community together, didn't they?" Lynn whispered, her voice wavering slightly as she dabbed at her eyes with a tissue.

"Yeah," Todd agreed, his throat tight with emotion. "They taught us all what love means."

As he spoke the words, a memory floated into his mind. A younger Jazz and Belle sat on a wooden porch swing, their fingers intertwined, their gazes locked onto one another's. They exchanged silent smiles, conveying their love without the need for words. The world around them seemed to fade away as if it were just the two– content, whole, and complete.

"Remember when they first got back together?" Todd asked, lost in the memory. "How they looked at each other like they'd found something they'd been searching for their entire lives, and we had no idea?"

Lynn nodded, tears brimming as the memory came to life before her. "I'll never forget it. It was like they breathed again after being underwater for too long."

The sun was casting a golden glow over the memorial service. Todd and Lynn stood side by side, united, as they greeted friends of Jazz and Belle, who had become like family over the years. The scent of fresh flowers filled the air, mingling with the crowd's soft murmurs.

"Your father taught me so much about music," said Mrs. Thompson, a petite woman with white hair pulled back into a neat bun. "I still remember the day he showed me how to play 'Moon River' on the piano."

"Jazz always loved that song," Todd replied, a smile tugging at the corners of his mouth. "He used to play it for Belle whenever he thought about it."

"Speaking of memories," Lynn chimed in, her eyes sparkling with mischief. "Did you hear the story of when Jazz and Belle accidentally set his parent's kitchen on fire while trying to make dinner together?"

Mrs. Thompson laughed, her eyes crinkling with warmth. "Oh, I do! Belle was always such a terrible cook back in those days. She always wanted to impress Jazz and bless her heart as she became a great cook. But they took it all in stride, didn't they?"

"Mom always said that memories were worth far more than material possessions," Lynn said, her voice thick with emotion. "She knew that even the messiest moments could bring joy if we allowed ourselves to see their beauty."

"And your father..." Mrs. Thompson turned to Todd, placing a comforting hand on his arm. "He never let his fading eyesight stop him from seeing the good in others. He was truly an inspiration to us all."

"Jazz taught me that it's not what we see with our eyes that matters, but what we feel in our hearts," Todd responded, his voice steady despite the tears threatening to spill over. "And I know they're still watching over us wherever they are now, guiding us with their love."

"Your parents' love was a beacon of hope for everyone in this town," Mrs. Thompson said, gently squeezing Todd's arm before releasing it. Thank you both for sharing them with us."

As the conversation flowed and laughter filled the air, the crowd seemed to shimmer with a sense of unity. The love Jazz had touched each person in attendance and Belle had shared, and their memories served as a testament to the enduring power of such a bond.

"Here's to Jazz and Belle," Lynn raised her glass in a toast, her voice carrying over the hum of conversation. "May their love continue to inspire us all."

"Cheers!" the group echoed, their voices lifting together in a joyful chorus that seemed to echo through the heavens where Jazz and Belle now resided. Their love continued to ripple into the world through every soul they touched.

As Todd's mind wandered, he found himself lost in memory about fifty years ago, when Jazz and Belle reunited after their time apart. Their love seemed to glow like a warm ember as they sat side by side on the porch of their small home, watching the sun dip below the horizon.

"Isn't it beautiful, Belle?" Jazz asked, his voice filled with awe at the sight before them.

Belle nodded, her blue eyes reflecting the brilliant colors of the sky. She reached over and gently squeezed Jazz's hand, a silent gesture that spoke volumes about their shared joy and enduring love.

Their knowing glances held a lifetime of memories, both the pain of separation and the overwhelming relief of finding their way back to each other. At that moment, the world around them seemed to dissolve, leaving only the two of them and the unbreakable bond they shared.

The scene shifted, bringing Todd back to the present. He stood beside Lynn in their home, surrounded by loved ones. The memorial service had ended, and friends and family had gathered in the warmth of their living room to share stories and remember Jazz and Belle.

"Jazz always said that the key to a happy marriage was laughter," said Uncle Mike, his voice thick with emotion as he recalled fond memories of his dear friends. "He told me that if you can laugh together, even through the tough times, you can weather any storm."

Lynn smiled softly at the memory, her eyes glistening with tears. "My mom used to write little notes for my dad and Jazz, with jokes or sweet messages. Even though she didn't speak often, she filled their lives with laughter and love."

"Speaking of laughter," Todd said, "I remember one time when Dad tried to surprise my mother when I was a little boy with breakfast in bed. He ended up tripping and accidentally dumped the entire tray onto the floor. You should've seen the look on his face!" The room erupted in laughter, the echoes of their joy paying tribute to Jazz and Belle's legacy of love.

"Both Jazz and Belle were truly remarkable," said Aunt Susan, her voice filled with admiration. "They taught all of us what it means to love unconditionally and to never give up on each other."

Todd glanced around the room, seeing Jazz and Belle's impact on everyone present. Their love had bound them all together like a tightly woven tapestry, each thread holding a cherished memory or lesson learned from the couple who had given so much.

"Thank you all for being here and remembering them," Todd said, his heart swelling with gratitude. "Jazz and Belle would be so pleased to know that their love lives on in every one of us."

Lynn reached for Todd's hand, giving it a gentle squeeze as they stood together, surrounded by the people they

loved and the memories they held dear. In that moment, they knew that the love Jazz and Belle had shared
would continue to guide and inspire them, both as
individuals and as a couple, for the rest of their lives.

The sun dipped below the horizon, painting the sky
with hues of pink and gold as the laughter of loved
ones filled the air. Todd and Lynn's backyard had transformed into a haven of heartfelt memories, each present
offering their tribute to Jazz and Belle through tales of
shared experiences.

"Remember that time we all went camping by the
lake?" Aunt Susan asked, her eyes twinkling with mischief. "Belle somehow managed to catch more fish than
all of us combined, even though she'd never fished a
day."

"Or when Jazz taught me how to ride a bike," chimed
in Cousin Mike, grinning from ear to ear. "I must've
fallen at least a dozen times, but he never let me give up.
By the end of the day, I was coasting along like a pro."

The montage of memories played out before them,
each story weaving together the threads that formed the
tapestry of Jazz and Belle's lives. From family vacations
exploring national parks to quiet afternoons curled up
on the porch with a good book, these moments defined
their love and brought joy to those around them.

"Hey, look what I found," said Lynn, gently pulling Todd away from the group. She held an old, worn photo album in her hands, its pages filled with pictures that captured the essence of Jazz and Belle's love story. Together, they sat down on a nearby bench, their fingers tracing the images of the past as they reminisced about the moments that had shaped their lives.

"Here's Belle and Jazz on the day they met," Todd murmured, his eyes softening as he gazed at the black-and-white photograph. "They looked so young and happy."

"And this one," Lynn said, pointing to a snapshot of Jazz and Belle dancing beneath a canopy of stars. "Remember how they'd sneak off to dance whenever they heard their favorite song playing? It was like the music called to their souls."

Each photograph revived a long-forgotten memory as they flipped through the album pages. There was Jazz teaching Todd how to fly a kite on a windy day, his arms wrapped protectively around his young son as they watched the bright colors soar high above them. And there was Belle, her face radiant with joy as she and Lynn gathered wildflowers in an open meadow, the petals shimmering like jewels in the sunlight.

"Thank you for finding this," Todd whispered, his voice thick with emotion as he looked into Lynn's watery eyes. "I had almost forgotten some of these moments."

Lynn leaned against him, her head resting on his shoulder as they journeyed through the past. "We were so blessed to have them, to learn from their love and wisdom. Their legacy lives on in us, and we'll ensure it continues for generations."

"Here's to Jazz and Belle," Todd said, raising an imaginary glass in tribute. "May their love light our path, always."

Lynn gently turned the page of the photo album, revealing a snapshot from decades ago: Jazz and Belle sitting on their porch swing, hands clasped together as they gazed out at the horizon. The serenity in their eyes told a story of love that had grown stronger with each passing day.

"Look at this one," Lynn murmured, her voice filled with wonder. "This is so close to how we found them that morning."

Todd leaned in closer, studying the photograph. He smiled wistfully. "It's like they knew even back then. They also wanted to be grandparents someday. They couldn't wait to share their love and wisdom with the next generation."

"Jazz used to say that if he had one wish, it would be for their legacy of love to live on after they were gone," Lynn added, her fingers tracing the outline of Belle's face in the picture.

"Let's make sure it does," Todd vowed, placing his hand over hers. They exchanged a determined glance before returning to the gathering of friends and family who had come to pay their respects to Jazz and Belle. Conversations had dwindled, replaced by a hushed silence as everyone waited for Todd and Lynn to speak.

"Everyone," Todd began, his voice steady yet laden with emotion. "We want to thank you all for being here today to celebrate our parents' lives, Jazz and Belle. Their love for each other was a beacon of light that guided us through even the darkest times."

Lynn nodded, taking a deep breath before continuing. "Their love taught us the true meaning of strength, compassion, and forgiveness. It showed us that when two people truly care for one another, no obstacle is too great or challenge is too daunting."

"Though Jazz and Belle are no longer with us, their love lives on," Todd said, his eyes glistening with unshed tears. "It lives on in the memories we share and the legacy they've left behind. We are eternally grateful for the wisdom they've imparted, the lessons they've taught, and the love they've given us."

"Let us raise a glass to Jazz and Belle," Lynn prompted, lifting her cup high. "To their unwavering love that will continue to guide and inspire us for generations."

"Here's to Jazz and Belle," echoed the crowd as glasses clinked together in a symphony of celebration and remembrance.

As the toast concluded and conversations resumed, Todd looked around at the faces of those whom Jazz and Belle's love had touched. A warmth emanated from deep within him, a tangible reminder of the enduring power of love. And though he knew that nothing could ever truly replace the presence of his father and mother-in-law, he also knew that their love would continue to live on - not just in his heart, but in the hearts of everyone who had been fortunate enough to know them.

The warm golden glow over the riverbank sparkled as the water sparkled with sunlight's reflection as it meandered peacefully through the town. This was one of Jazz and Belle's favorite places, where they had spent countless hours basking in the sun, laughing, and sharing their love for each other.

"Can you believe how many people are here?" Todd asked Lynn. His voice filled with awe as he surveyed the crowd, which was there to celebrate Jazz and Belle's love.

"Jazz and Belle touched so many lives," Lynn replied affectionately, her eyes shining. It's incredible to see everyone come together like this."

And indeed, it was a sight to behold. Children laughed and played games by the water's edge while adults danced and swayed to the gentle melodies that filled the air. Family members and friends shared stories of Jazz and Belle, their laughter filling the air like the sweetest songs.

"Remember that time when Jazz tried to teach Belle to fish?" Todd chuckled, recalling the memory fondly. "He insisted it was a rite of passage, but she just pretended she couldn't get the hang of it."

"Of course, I remember!" Lynn laughed. "But what about how Belle could simply sit by the water, listen, and somehow bring peace to anyone who joined her? She didn't need words to make you feel loved and understood."

The crowd quieted down and made their way toward the community center. A large plaque bearing an inscription that captured the essence of Jazz and Belle's love had been placed on one of its walls.

"Let us gather in gratitude and remembrance," said Todd, gesturing towards the plaque. "For it is through these words that we honor the hearts of Jazz and Belle."

"Love knows no boundaries, nor does it fade with time," the plaque read. "It lives on in our hearts, a beacon of hope and light for all whose warmth has touched. In memory of Jazz Montgomery and Belle Thompson, whose love has forever enriched our lives."

A collective sigh of contentment and peace washed over the crowd as they took in words, each reflecting upon how Jazz and Belle's love had shaped their lives.

"May their love continue to inspire us, even in their absence," Lynn whispered, her hand finding Todd's as they stood side by side.

"Forever and always," Todd agreed, squeezing her hand gently.

As the evening drew to a close, the joy and unity that had filled the air at the riverbank lingered like a warm embrace. Jazz and Belle's legacy lived on, not just in the hearts of Todd and Lynn but also in everyone who had gathered to celebrate their enduring love. And though their physical presence was missed, their love would continue to serve as a guiding light—a beacon of hope, warmth, and inspiration for future generations.

A light rain fell over the cemetery, its soft pattern providing a soothing backdrop to the moment. Todd and Lynn stood with their children, Jazzy and Bella, in front of Jazz and Belle's shared headstone. The engraved names testified to the enduring love that once flourished in their grandparents' hearts.

"Here we are again, kids," Lynn said gently, her eyes misting over as she held a bundle of letters. "Your grandparents wrote these to each other, and they're filled with so much love."

"Even though they're not here anymore, we want you to know about their beautiful love story," Todd added, his strong jawline quivering slightly. "Let's read some of them together."

As they read aloud the heartfelt words exchanged between Jazz and Belle, Jazzy and Bella listened intently, their young faces reflecting their deep connection to their namesakes.

"Jazz wrote here that Belle was 'the one who made him see life in technicolor,'" Lynn recited, her voice full of emotion.

"Listen to this part," Todd continued, eyes scanning another letter. "'And though my eyesight fades, our love remains a beacon of hope, bringing light to even the darkest of corners.'"

"Wow," Jazzy whispered, his hand reaching out to trace the engraved names on the headstone. "I wish I could've met them."

"Me too," Bella agreed, her blue eyes shimmering with unshed tears.

"Though you never got the chance to meet them, their love lives on through us," Lynn said softly, pulling her children close. "And it's something we'll always share as a family."

"Speaking of sharing," Todd said, wiping away a stray tear. "You two wrote a poem for your grandparents, didn't you?"

With determined nods, Jazzy and Bella stepped forward, their tiny hands clutching the paper that held the words they had poured their hearts into.

"Dear Grandma Belle and Grandpa Jazz, we never met, but we feel your love so much," Jazzy began, his voice clear despite the raindrops falling around them.

"Your legacy of love will continue to grow through us, your grandchildren, who love you so," Bella continued, her voice strong and steady.

"Even though we're apart, your love is our guide, a light in our hearts where you'll always reside," they finished together, their words echoing across the cemetery.

Todd and Lynn exchanged proud glances before embracing Jazzy and Bella, their hearts swelling with gratitude for the love they had learned from Jazz and Belle. As the rain continued to fall, each droplet seemed to carry the unbreakable connection between past and present, weaving together a tapestry of love that spanned generations.

"Remember, kids," Lynn whispered, her eyes locked on the headstone. "Their love story is now part of our love story, and we'll keep it alive – forever and always."

The End

www.ingramcontent.com/pod-product-compliance
Lightning Source LLC
Chambersburg PA
CBHW050854150626
46549CB00013B/1715